Hermann KAUFMANN

Spirit of Nature Wood Architecture Award 2010

Hermann KAUFMANN

Spirit of Nature Wood Architecture Award 2010

RAKENNUSTIETO PUBLISHING

PUBLISHER	Wood in Culture Association
	Salomonkatu 17 A
	00100 Helsinki, Finland
	tel. +358 9 6850 8841
	fax +358 9 6850 8820
	woodinculture@smy.fi
PUBLISHING COMPANY	Rakennustieto Publishing
GRAPHIC DESIGN	Anders Adlercreutz
LAYOUT AND IMAGE EDITING	Rakennustieto
TRANSLATIONS	Foreword: Heli Mäntyniemi (Finnish–English); Industrial Architecture Born from Intelligent Handicraft: Josbel Oy (German–Finnish); Gekko/ Gareth Griffiths, Kristina Kölhi (Finnish–English); Projects: Andrea Lyman, Mark Gilbert, Pedro M. López (German–English), Josbel Oy (German–Finnish); Outi Leinonen (English–Finnish); Gareth Griffiths and Kristina Kölhi (Finnish–English); Further information see p. 144
LANGUAGE CONSULTING	Gareth Griffiths (English)
EDITOR	Kristiina Lehtimäki / Rakennustieto (Finnish texts)
PHOTOGRAPHS	Nikolaus Walter, Adolf Bereuter, Ignacio Martinez, Bruno Klomfar, Hermann Kaufmann, Werner Huthmacher
PAPER	Gallerie Art Silk 150 g m^2
ISBN	978-951-682-965-7 (this edition)
	978-951-682-966-4 (Finnish edition)
PRINTERS	Kariston Kirjapaino Oy, Hämeenlinna 2010
©	Wood in Culture Association, Hermann Kaufmann and Rakennustieto Oy

Rakennustieto
www.rakennustieto.fi
P.O. Box 1004
00101 Helsinki, Finland
phone + 358 207 476 400

contents

Foreword   6

Naming the Winner   8

Industrial Architecture Born
from Intelligent Handicraft   10

Zerlauth House   16
Frastanz, Vorarlberg, Austria, 2003

Olperer Shelter   22
Zillertal, Tyrol, Austria, 2007

Bicycle Bridge   28
Gaissau, Vorarlberg, Austria, 1999

Elma Alp Vacation Home   34
Mellental, Mellau, Austria, 2005

Mühlweg Housing Estate   42
Vienna, Austria, 2006

Ölzbündt Housing Estate   50
Dornbirn, Vorarlberg, Austria, 1997

MM Immobilien St. Georgen
GmbH Offices   56
St. Georgen, Attergau, Austria, 2008

Office and Residential
Building Sportplatzweg   64
Schwarzach, Vorarlberg, Austria, 1999

Ludesch Community Centre   72
Ludesch, Vorarlberg, Austria, 2005

Sutterlüty Supermarket   80
Weiler, Vorarlberg, Austria, 2002

Metzler Timber Warehouse and Offices   84
Bezau, Vorarlberg, Austria, 1995

Sohm Holzbau Office and Industrial
Building, Extension   90
Alberschwende, Vorarlberg, Austria, 2009

Wälderhaus Industrial Park   96
Bezau, Vorarlberg, Austria, 2002

Rheinhof Estate   102
Hohenems, Vorarlberg, Austria, 2006

St. Gerold Riding Hall   108
St. Gerold, Vorarlberg, Austria, 1997

Mehrerau Gymnasium, Conversion   116
Mehrerau, Bregenz, Vorarlberg, Austria, 1997

Adler Inn, Renovation   122
Schwarzenberg, Vorarlberg, Austria

Mesmers Stable, Conversion   126
Alberschwende, Vorarlberg, Austria, 2004

Project Information   135

FOREWORD

LAURI TARASTI
Chair of the Advisory Committee, Wood in Culture Association

JUHA MÄNTYLÄ
Chair of the Board, Finnish Forest Foundation

FINNISH FOREST FOUNDATION

Forest and wood have always played an important role in Finnish culture and daily life. Whatever the purpose, the use of wood begins with planning and design. In the choice of construction materials, too, the influence of architecture and design is decisive.

The popularity of wood as a construction material has for a number of reasons increased in recent years: it is versatile and visually attractive, and new innovative wood products have enabled new construction solutions. At the same time, the environmental friendliness of forestry and wood processing, and especially the small carbon footprint of the overall production chain, have increased the reputation of wood as an ecological material. In the case of Finland, wood is also a domestic material.

The international Spirit of Nature Wood Architecture Award is granted for architectural achievements to an individual or group demonstrating a skilled and creative use of wood in their work. The Award is presented every second year. The first Award was given in 2000 to Italian architect Renzo Piano. The subsequent recipients have been architects Kengo Kuma from Japan (2002), Richard Leplastrier from Australia (2004), Peter Zumthor from Switzerland (2006) and José Cruz Ovalle from Chile (2008).

The recipient of the international Spirit of Nature Wood Architecture Award is selected by a jury, whose members in 2010 were architects Matti Rautiola (Chair), Samuli Miettinen and Unto Siikanen from Finland and Ingerid Helsing Almaas from Norway. The Award of EUR 40,000 is presented on 10th September 2010 in connection with a concert at the Sibelius Festival held at the Sibelius Hall in Lahti.

The recipient of the 2010 international Spirit of Nature Wood Architecture Award is architect and professor of architecture Hermann Kaufmann from Austria. He has a long and distinguished career as a designer and teacher. During the last 25 years, Kaufmann has designed various new buildings, ranging from family residences to riding halls, from chapels to community centres and blocks of flats, as well as numerous renovation and remodelling projects. 85 % of his production is based on the use of wood.

For the first time ever, this year the Young Spirit of Nature Wood Architecture Award is being presented. Its purpose is to encourage students of architecture studying in Finland to be creative in the use of wood as well as to promote new talent. The Award of EUR 5,000 is presented for a final thesis in architecture in which wood has a central role.

The recipient of the first Young Spirit of Nature Award is Sanna Jokimäki. Her Master's thesis, "Views on Prefabricated Modular Architecture, School Construction as an Implementation", was completed in 2010 at the School of Architecture at Tampere University of Technology.

The Wood in Culture Association wishes to express its gratitude to the Finnish Forest Foundation for providing the support that enables the distribution of the Awards. In particular, we would like to commend the Foundation's initiative in establishing the Young Spirit of Nature Wood Architecture Award. The simultaneous presentation of awards to an international master and a skilled young professional creates a new dialogue; the award winners are the best in their field and their work serves as a paragon for others.

Our warmest gratitude is also due to the members of the Jury for their active work, which this year required plenty of time and study since they had to deliberate on two awards. Further, we would like to thank our partners who have assisted in many ways with arranging the events related to the award presentation and thus contributed to the promotion of high-class wood construction.

ELMA ALP VACATION HOME. PHOTO: BRUNO KLOMFAR

NAMING
THE WINNER

MATTI RAUTIOLA

Professor, Architect SAFA
Chairman of the Jury

The Spirit of Nature Wood Architecture Award is one of the most prestig-
ious architecture prizes in the world and the only significant international
recognition for wood architecture. This year the Award is being presented
for the sixth time. The five previous recipients have come from four different continents and represent both pioneers of wood architecture and
new masters with emerging careers on the world scene.

In 2010 the focus has turned back to Europe yet again. The winner of
the Award, architect Hermann Kaufmann, lives and works in Vorarlberg
in Austria, in the area where he was born and where his family, relatives and collaborators also live. He has a long career in wood architecture, preserving and renewing the tradition of wood workmanship, and
working together closely with local professionals. After his studies in
Innsbruck and Vienna and a couple of years of practise he founded in
1983 an office together with Christian Lenz. The team he works with has
grown over the years to a total of some 20 people. The commissions are
mainly in Vorarlberg but their expertise and know-how are increasingly
requested also outside the region, elsewhere in Austria and abroad. The
gallery of work consists of wooden buildings in all scales and categories;
from small-scale restorations of old utility buildings and restaurants
to private houses, apartment blocks, community centres and industrial
buildings – all of them almost entirely wood constructions. Over the
years he has shared his valuable knowledge with students in several
universities, and since 2002 he has been a professor of architecture at
Munich Technical University.

Hermann Kaufmann has devoted his career to the research and development of wood construction and building processes. The inspiration for the
work comes from a deep respect for the local tradition, local workman-

ship, small-sized enterprises and workshops and the generations-long understanding of how to build with wood in a harsh climate. The long distances, harsh winters and isolated villages have led to a production structure, a network, which is based on small units and collaboration. Undoubtedly, the building culture has led to shared responsibility for vocational education, and a high ambition and societal unity, a way of surviving and succeeding together. Such a great tradition and values continue to show in Hermann Kaufmann's work.

The challenges of building in the mountains have inspired Kaufmann to develop prefabrication techniques. Massive wooden slabs have solved the problem of achieving long spans with wood construction. The massive wood partition wall solutions have proven to be practical, durable and economical.

Energy efficiency and healthy structures have always been in the focus of Kaufmann's work. His first passive houses were constructed already in the 1990s. The applications were then extended to multi-storey apartment buildings. The notable fact is that, despite high-performance structures, the buildings are affordable, easy to maintain and beautiful architecture.

Hand in hand with Kaufmann's societal awareness and humble responsibility goes the subtle modernism of his buildings. The caring presence of the architecture lives in harmony with the tradition, expressing a thorough consideration for that tradition, and uncompromising finishing. The perfection in the detailing is admirable, based on functionality, durability and sensitive materiality, the delight of the hand. This can only be realised with seamless collaboration between the architect and the builders. The bridge between the new and the old is built of the material, its surface and treatment, scale, patterns and traditional methods of working, that the skilful and ambitious carpenters carry on over generations.

Vorarlberg has developed into a functioning network of small and medium sized enterprises. It takes care of the education of future professionals, creates and follows its own quality standards, competes internally yet simultaneously collaborates in versatile combinations. Smallness, quickness and flexibility have become competitive factors that help in adapting different sized projects. In the end it is no surprise that the area has not experienced any economic recession. On the contrary, the cluster has generated welfare and prosperity for the whole area.

On behalf of the Jury I wish to thank Hermann Kaufmann and his collaborators for all their amicable guidance and help, both during the jury's visit to Austria and when making this book. Hermann Kaufmann builds from wood, sustainably and beautifully, with the people and for the people. The Spirit of Nature Wood Architecture Award is a tribute to his career and work, the value of which extends over decades and borders.

The Award has been made possible by the Wood in Culture Association. Their remarkable support for wood architecture and its promotion has helped us in making the world a bit better place.

INDUSTRIAL ARCHITECTURE BORN FROM INTELLIGENT HANDICRAFT

OTTO KAPFINGER

Vienna, Austria

Hermann Kaufmann is a pioneer in contemporary European wood construction. He comes from a family of carpentry and wood industry professionals from the federal state of Vorarlberg, an area of Austria known for decades above all for its innovative wood construction. Kaufmann has achieved a key position in the internationally respected field of wood construction because the different aspects of planning, development and design in wood industry and the wood technology converge in him and his personal and professional environment in an almost ideal way.

His father, Ernst Kaufmann, worked as a carpenter in the village of Reuthe in Bregenzerwald. His grandfather, Josef Kaufmann, was the founder of Holzbauwerk Kaufmann, which became the largest wood-processing and wood construction company for glulam products in the region. His uncle, Leopold Kaufmann, who lived in the nearby town of Bezau, was one of the first generation from the so-called "Vorarlberg school of Architecture", which already in the 1960s combined the local carpentry tradition with the design of unique projects, and in doing so began to renew tradition. His brothers Michael, Ernst and Johannes, naturally enough, also work in the field, as manufacturers, enterprisers and designers. Drawing from this extensive network of experiences of both handicrafts and material and production technology, Hermann Kaufmann has since the mid-1980s developed industrially-produced wood construction by creating new types of load-bearing structures, and has also been a pioneer in the careful renewal of old wooden buildings and energy-optimized ecological building.

A particularly decisive aspect in the incredible success of the "Vorarlberg school of Architecture" has been that its projects have not been academic creations, but rather have been created in cooperation between young and enthusiastic people – most of them low wage earners and searching for apartments – housing cooperatives and clients. In other words, what has been particularly decisive is the fact that this architectural revolution was not dictated from above but directed from the lower strata of society in opposition to prevailing customs, so that these people themselves were able to participate. Thus what is particularly characteristic of Hermann

Kaufmann, who belongs to the second generation of the "Vorarlberg school of Architecture", is that his wooden buildings do not come about at the architect's drawing table or computer, but rather always begin with the material itself, the workshop, the building site, and the basic principles and opportunities of a wood building technology that is able to develop and remain economically competitive.

Kaufmann himself sees his roots specifically in the handicraft tradition of Bregenzerwald – not so much in the tradition of historical forms but in the proven spiritual capital. "Handicraft is a school for thinking," he says, "and as such it is the best and most durable: it teaches us concretely, ruthlessly, and in an incredible way, to follow precisely the material-technological logic, in other words, the basics of good workmanship – *how* and *from what* something is made, and it also teaches us cultural-technical wisdom, the applied principles of sensible workmanship and design – *why* and *for what purpose* something is made. The structural doctrine of handicraft is intimately connected to the dialogue with the material: the suitability of each and every technical and formal choice is assessed in the manufacturing and functional processes immediately and exactly – not only at the present moment but also in the future. One must continuously consider how each idea and each new or altered use influences the entire know-how, and then reinforces, improves, expands, and establishes it in many future uses. Handicraft teaches us additionally about the intelligent economy of the consumption, working and use of the material – the intention is to achieve a maximal result, a maximal performance, with as little consumption as possible. Everything in the ethics of handicraft that requires or leads to waste becomes obsolete. On the contrary, the greatest pleasure, genuine efficiency and beauty come about when the product is genuinely 'intelligent' and designed, thought through and cleverly realised with respect to the aforementioned values. A good craftsman does not draw his ideas from the continuous repetition of what has already been proven to work, but remains active and oriented towards the future by continuously undertaking considered experimentation – not for the sake of experimentation but purposefully from a concrete starting point, with the intention to optimise, develop and differentiate the whole system. Looked at in this way, handicraft is an evolutionary system invented and developed by man, which is parallel to the evolutionary processes of nature. There is nothing new here, these subjects have been recognised long ago by well-known architects and technical and cultural reformers. I have suckled this in my mother's milk, from the many discussions with my father and uncle, from the everyday presence of the wood industry enterprises of my relatives, and from the still visible practical life of the mountain peasants of our own area, Bregenzerwald."

Architect and university professor Ernst Hiesmayr, a person greatly respected by Hermann Kaufmann, has stated: "The level of culture is the joint product of the community, craftsmen and designers. The craftsmen have always used the world's natural resources extremely frugally. They are the ecological models of the future." Hiesmayr has also explained the success of the new "Vorarlberg school of Architecture" as follows: "Due to people's sense of reality, the architects and the receptive middle classes, development has taken place despite stubborn resistance. Artisan architecture has been created rather than artistic architecture put together in experimental laboratories. In this way, the connections to tradition have been successful, while not forgetting modern-day life."

There have always been several decisive factors in the new wooden architecture of Vorarlberg that are connected to the renewal of the whole wood technology: firstly, from the 1960s onwards, architects had spoken in favour of rational wood frame building, so that self-build construction would become possible, particularly for young clients; secondly, in the beginning of the 1970s, an environmental movement was born in the region which also sought construction alternatives and took a slightly deeper interest than people elsewhere in solar-energy building, natural building materials and the careful utilization of the climate, natural resources and landscape (a third of the area of the federal state is forest!)

Hermann Kaufmann began his career at the very moment when the projects of so-called "Baukünstler" received a more widely approved professional acceptance, so that from 1985-86 onwards also heating efficiency calculations and industrial wood construction techniques were made use of, and also carpenters and timber producers began on their own initiative to strengthen the position of contemporary materials and structures and to develop them themselves. In 1985 an energy research institute was established in Dornbirn and the first solar-energy house was built in Lauterach in the district of Bregenz. In 1987-90 Hermann Kaufmann, together with Sture Larsen and Walter Unterrainer, built a school in Dafins, the first solar-energy public building in Austria. The building has an insulated wood frame construction with the whole of the south facade functioning as a solar heat-collector, and with a gravel storage system and hypocaust system in the internal walls. Also at that time, Kaufman created (together with Christian Lenz) new industrial wood applications by developing large-sized bearing structures suitable for industrial buildings for Holzbauwerk Kaufmann, as well as for the workshop of his brother, Michael Kaufmann, and for several large parish halls.

In 1990 began a politically sanctioned era in state-subsidized housing production in Vorarlberg, where there was a promotion and official technical coding of ecological building. The subsidised energy-saving housing then had to meet the annual heating-energy requirement of 60 kWh/m2a. That same year Kaufmann and Unterrainer built a semi-detached house in Lustenau, in which a trombe wall was integrated into the completely glazed south facades and which had a hypocaust heating system. After this Kaufmann built a semi-detached house in Dornbirn where the annual heating energy requirement was 53 kWh/m2a; thus the well-insulated prefabricated wooden elements, and the untreated larch boarding of the façades (which were protected by an overhanging roof) paved the way for the design of the Ölzbündt housing block in Dornbirn, completed in 1997. If the early wooden buildings of Kaufmann were given a new appearance in terms of the interiors and technology and where modular

and untreated wood frame constructions were used, then around 1995 the technology changed as CNC machining became more common among the various enterprises in the field, who began to manufacture large-sized and extensive prefabricated elements.

Wood construction has always required extremely precise and versatile planning and implementation. With industrialisation, wood had been replaced by other building materials, but with the changing trend towards environmentally-conscious building wood construction technology again became topical. The CO_2-neutral, locally available raw material – by its very nature renewable – created the basis for this alternative that takes into account the future situation. Also in its way influential was the development of glulam. Its affordable price guaranteed availability, it was available in different shaped industrial products, and it allowed for increasingly precise and flexible combinations and computer-guided handling. Also the development of the materials based on solid wood (e.g. cross-laminated timber) and improvements of the jointing techniques by using double threaded screws improved the structural mechanics of wood construction and made instalment easier, more precise and quicker. Seen from these and other viewpoints, the timber industry enterprises, carpenters and architects of Vorarlberg have, by international standards, achieved a beneficial position. They have established new norms and have in synergy with local forestry, saw mills, testing institutions, structural engineers, fire-safety experts, local government and marketing experts, developed their own product area.

In both the regional and inter-regional environment, the importance of the Ölzbündt apartment block, designed by Hermann Kaufmann in 1996-97, has been unique. The owner of the plot, graphic artist Gerold Ölz, together with Anton Kaufmann, Hermann Kaufmann's cousin, director of Holzbauwerk Kaufmann, constructed the building, containing 13 apartments and an atelier, in just 18 weeks. Placed on top of an underground parking hall is a prefabricated wooden so-called "table construction": using a building frame module of 2,40 x 4,8 metres; the hollow roof and intermediate floor

NIKOLAUS WALTER

elements are supported on columns and filled to achieve soundproofing; the bathrooms and kitchens were preassembled in the factory; and there are heavily-insulated and sealed prefabricated elements for the exterior walls. The balconies and walkways are lightweight steel and wood constructions fixed to the main building frame of the larch-wood clad building. The adjustable ventilation with geo-thermal heat exchange, heat recovery from extracted air, and additional heating by means of a heat pump, together guarantee for each apartment fresh air intake that is individually heated and thus replaces traditional heating systems. Despite the fact that the building cost the same to build as a comparable conventional project, as well as the numerous awards it has received and its numerous appearances in publications, the Ölzbündt apartment block was for a long time a unique case. The quality of the building had been achieved because the expert local major enterprise had taken care of every aspect of the project; from the design and factory fabrication all the way to construction, and the building was considered a kind of show house, and a calling card. In normal social housing projects, on the other hand, all the different stages of the work have to go undergo tender bids and the work must be awarded to the company that offers the cheapest bid. Thus, from the point of view of ensuring quality, the amount of work required for proper coordination is disproportionate and more laborious and the quality of the different sub-areas also differs considerably. For the construction of residential buildings in Wolfurt, Telfs, Schwarzach, and elsewhere, Kaufmann lowered the overall standards so that every carpenter would be able to meet them.

The next ground-breaking building was a new community centre in Ludesch, completed in 2005. The municipality, with a population of 3000, had already for some time invested in energy saving and sustainable development. The aim was to build an architectonically high-quality and ecological demonstration project for commercial premises and apartments in such a way that the citizens of the town could have an influence on the project.

Hermann Kaufmann's versatile and practical experience and, beyond any quantifiable values, his masterly command of the aesthetical and spatial art aspects of construction are superbly evident in the examples presented here. Also the 43-metre long bicycle and pedestrian bridge in Gaissau, which has been built completely from a prefabricated wooden construction with integrated steel cables, seems at first glance, and particularly in photos, to be rather simple. On visiting the site, however, the bridge construction turns out to be a complex spatial artwork that reacts sensitively to the local conditions.

The strength of the building industry in Vorarlberg lay and still lies in its understanding of structural concepts, creating space from the structure, the materials, and the use itself. The secret to the success and uniqueness of this architecture was and still is partly that people do not want anything special or fancy, but rather ideal conditions for everyday life. Hermann Kaufmann is an excellent representative of this field and viewpoint. His comprehensive professional skill, the starting point of which lies in wood handicrafts, does not begin or end with beautiful architecture, but he defines contemporary building as part of a responsible consideration for the environment, landscape, natural resources and biosphere. "As versatile as is necessary and as simple as possible" is a motto that Walter Zschokke has associated with the architecture of this multi-award-winning, international expert and professor of wood building. Kaufmann himself succinctly encapsulates this sorely longed for architectural synthesis of handicraft-industrial technology and sustainable development that has become so difficult today: "I come from a craftsman family and I am an architect who feels more at home in the workshop and on the building site than in the studio and at a drawing table. The interaction of these two worlds operates as follows: the architect sees that the simple does not become banal and the craftsman sees that the simple does not become complex."

projects

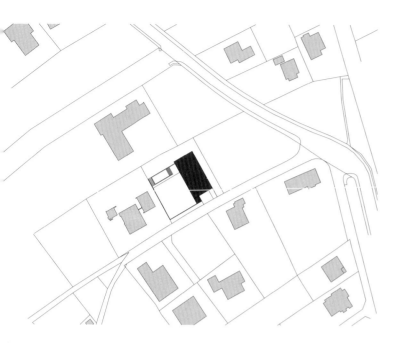

ZERLAUTH HOUSE

Frastanz, Vorarlberg, Austria, 2003

Text: Otto Kapfinger

The small town of Frastanz, near Feldkirch, between the Rhine Valley and the Arlberg mountain range, is home to a large number of businesses. In contrast to the Bregenzerwald region, this area is firmly in the grip of a globalized present. Here a flat roof no longer prompts a debate on style, and swimming pools have become a common phenomenon – even when they are as extravagant as the one accompanying this house.

The house is situated on the urban periphery, densely surrounded by other structures. The view to the west extends to the Swiss Alps. Access to the house is from the east side, which is the highest point on the site, from where one enters the living space, which seamlessly connects to the garden on the south side. The garden is delineated by walls on two sides and borders the pool, which marks a variation in the terrain on the northwest side.

The gentle slope allowed for the placement of the bedrooms in the basement, which is lit from the west side. The building seeks to offer a sense of security, whilst also opening up to the garden and the view. The design was further determined by the form of the roof connecting to the north-east wall: synthesizing in a single gesture privacy and transparency. Energy consumption is very low, despite the wide expanses of glass. Heating and ventilation are coupled with heat recovery, and hot water is generated by solar collectors.

The architecture of Vorarlberg is often compared to "boxes", but Frastanz is the antithesis: open rooms under a roof, abstracted to form a spatial angle.

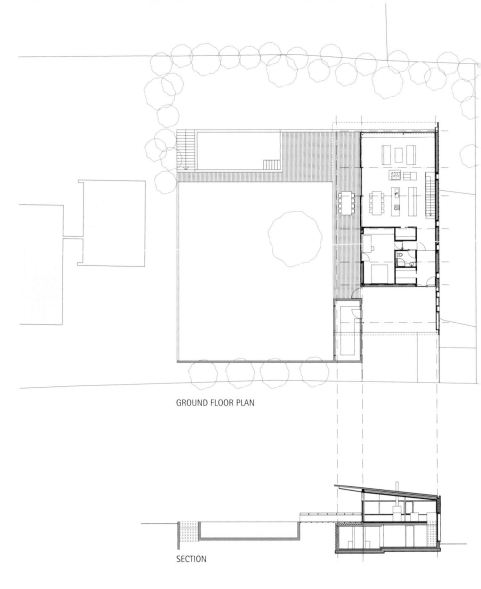

GROUND FLOOR PLAN

SECTION

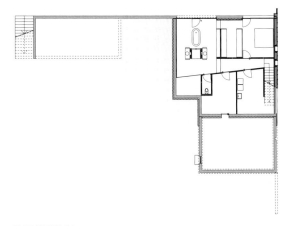

BASEMENT PLAN

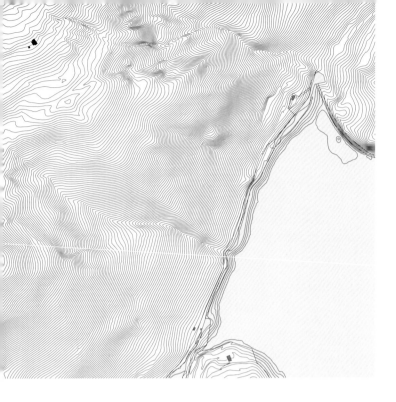

OLPERER SHELTER

Zillertal, Tyrol, Austria, 2007

Text: Otto Kapfinger

For more than a hundred years, a shelter had been standing at this exposed location high above the "Schlegeisspeicher" reservoir, opposite which are the glaciers and mountain tops of the Zillertal Alps. Since refurbishment of the old building was deemed impossible, in 2005 the decision was made to build a new one, and Hermann Kaufmann's office, with its entry titled "Innovation through simplicity", won the invited architectural competition. In Kaufmann's own words: "High altitude construction did and still does depend on the availability of transportation. The old hut was built from stone from the surrounding area. The transportation of large quantities of construction material from the valley was not feasible in those days; labour-intensive stone masonry was cheaper. Modern means of transportation, such as the helicopter, have changed things. Prefabricated construction materials, together with the new possibilities provided by glulam timber allow for easy transportation. Furthermore, they can be quickly assembled, which is an important aspect in high altitude construction. In addition, the physical qualities of timber allow for direct and optimal ecological construction. The glulam timber panels have good load-bearing and insulation properties. Additional insulation was not required because the shelter is open only during the summertime. This entirely timber structure without insulation, cladding, etc. can – plainly spoken – just rot up there on its spot. Due to the harsh weather conditions, we have shingled the outer surfaces and within a few years the greyed wood will have entered into a dialogue with the surrounding world of stone."

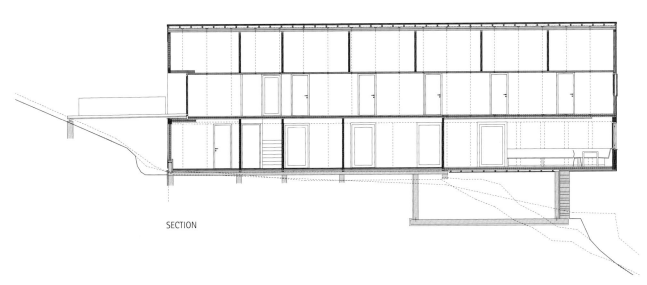

SECTION

Kaufmann deliberately designed the shelter as a refuge and not as a hotel. It is a summer shelter; the comfort is commensurate with the expectations reasonable for such a location. The entrance hall and bedrooms are unheated. The building utilities are limited to a minimum; a stove and the heat from a photovoltaic and canola oil-powered CHP installation used for water purification supply the building with heat. The project's motto of "innovation through reduction" is already reflected in its typological approach. The old building has been replaced by a compact structure with a pitched roof, cantilevered over a retaining wall and facing the reservoir. The concrete base, which has been clad with stone from the surrounding area, has been backfilled with rubble from the demolished hut, while the building structure itself is built from spruce glulam. The outer walls of the ground floor act as support plates and are hinge jointed to the base in order to reduce the load on the cantilever. Mounted on these cantilevers is the large panorama window of the gable wall. Suspended from this in turn are the floor plates for the restaurant section. Bracing is provided by the floor plate and the roof, which also act as a stabilising slabs. A small, auxiliary building (with additional thermal insulation) serves as a wintertime shelter and accommodation for self-caterers.

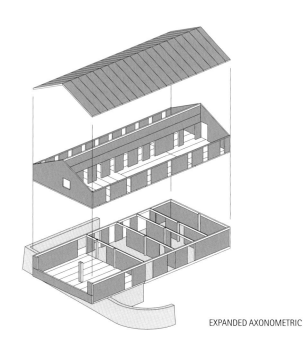

EXPANDED AXONOMETRIC

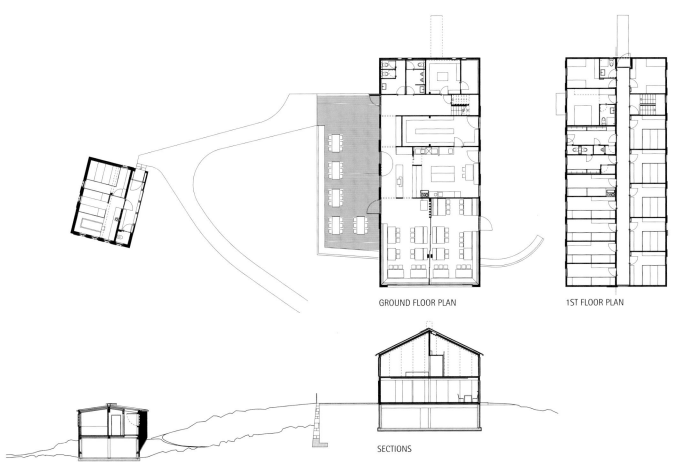

GROUND FLOOR PLAN

1ST FLOOR PLAN

SECTIONS

BICYCLE BRIDGE

Gaissau, Altes Zollamt, Vorarlberg, Austria, 1999
Text: Hermann Kaufmann Office

The two main supports of the bridge are of an unusual construction. They consist of two separate pairs of glulam beams (each with a section 130 cm x 10 cm), one above the other. Between them are five vertical steel compression members and two tension members consisting of four flat steel rods. Because the roof of the bridge is horizontal but the bike route itself tilted, the parabolas commonly used in tensioning members could not be used. Every curve in the tensioning member creates approximately 1000 kN of lateral force in the wooden joints, which is difficult to control with tensile force.

The main problem turned out to be directing the force from the tensioning member to the upper compression member. By widening the tensioning member at the ends, the force was evenly spread through the cross section of the wood structure.

Below the level of the cycle route is a horizontal steel girder frame. The roof, constructed from 40 mm sandwich board, functions as a shear panel, and must, in addition to its normal task, ensure the stability of the upper beam.

A HEB 320 steel girder has been fastened at each end of the bridge, which directs the lateral forces to the bearings, thus stabilising the bridge construction.

The supports between the glulam beams have been attached to the joints of the bicycle bridge, supporting the roof and preventing the tilting of the narrow rods.

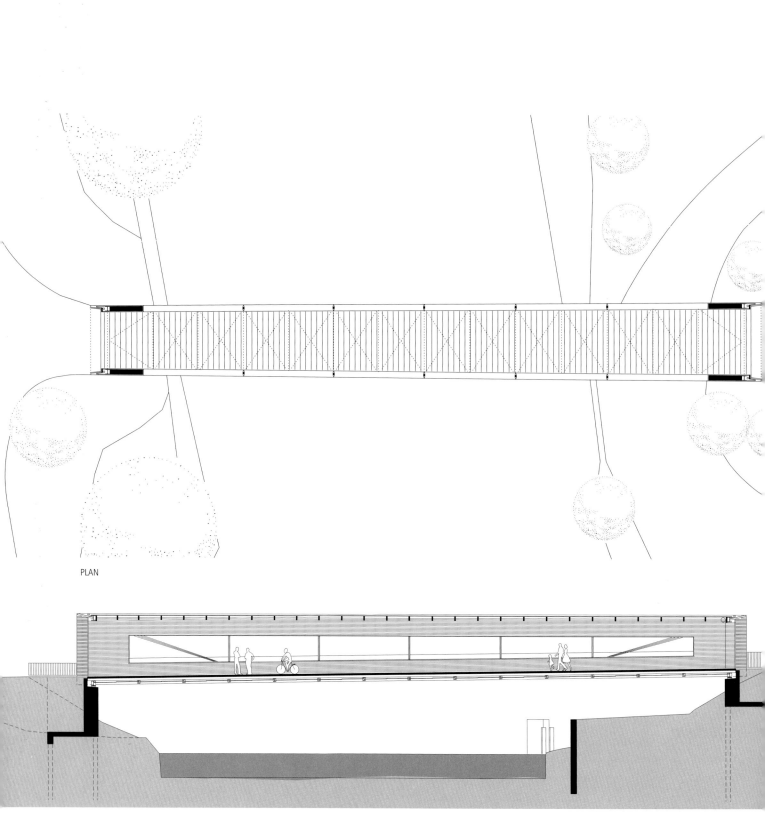

PLAN

SECTION

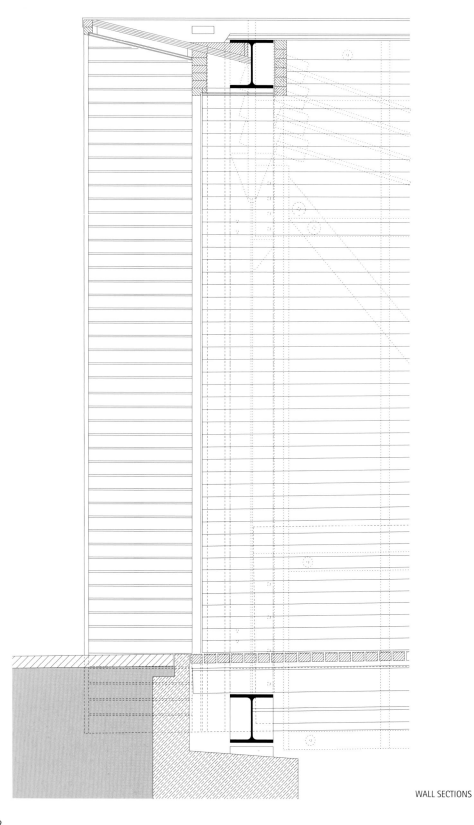

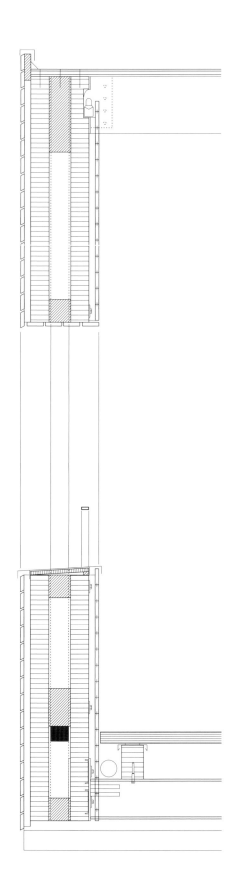

WALL SECTIONS

ELMA ALP
VACATION HOME

Mellental, Mellau, Austria, 2005
Text: Otto Kapfinger

In the Bregenzerwald region, pastures for livestock are used in three seasonal cycles. This tradition gave rise to the so-called "Vorsäß", an alpine homestead at an altitude around 1000 metres, to which animals were brought twice a year – in spring and autumn – for 4–5 weeks. Alpine farmers owned ten cows at most, and as a result the Vorsäß chalets were typically very small and modestly equipped for short stays.

Simplicity is one of the central features of these Alpine structures, and their pure and natural atmosphere makes them popular vacation homes. When building the Elma Vorsäß in Mellental, the architect sought to capture this special atmosphere. He used only timber as the building material, minimized the proportions of the spaces and introduced a stripped-down floor plan, the anchoring point for which is the fireplace in the centre of the building. The building has no additional thermal insulation and is made entirely of solid wood; the roof structure is built of solid wood boards.

Inspired by traditional forms, the house also boasts newly interpreted details – horizontal sliding windows, ample glazing in the living room and an open cross-section – in line with modern standards of living. The ground floor and common area are built with vertically arranged timber studs, so as to avoid any settling of the backfilling, which could damage the sliding windows. The upper floor, containing the bedrooms, is built with horizontal beams, with modern edge joints – blind dovetail joints cut with a CNC mill. The dovetail joints allow for the beams to interlock at corners with no gap between them. Consequently, the end grain is not exposed to weathering. Spotless surfaces were not a priority, thus no varnish, coating or tiling were used. From the ridge-beam to the furniture, everything is made of locally sourced, untreated solid wood.

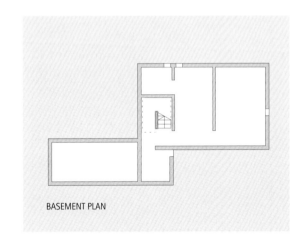

BASEMENT PLAN

1ST FLOOR PLAN

GROUND FLOOR PLAN

ATTIC FLOOR PLAN

MÜHLWEG HOUSING ESTATE

Vienna, Austria, 2006

Cooperation with Johannes Kaufmann Architektur

Text: Otto Kapfinger

In 2003, the Vienna Land Procurement and Urban Renewal Fund invited tenders for the "timber and mixed-timber construction" of a residential complex with 250 apartments. In the context of the "Climate Protection Program of the City of Vienna", the city intended to demonstrate the feasibility of energy-efficient timber structures built as affordable housing for urban sites. The recent amendment of the local building regulations had paved the way for multi-storey timber structures to be subsidized in the the city's social housing program.

The winning proposal in the public competition was designed by Johannes and Hermann Kaufmann. Their design provided for a clearly structured, spatially site-specific and highly differentiated link between the residential buildings from the 1960s to the west and the green space to the east. The proximity to the plot boundaries and the arrangement of the volumes provide for an inner courtyard area which, despite its clear structure, is open to its environs. Thus, the transition to the landscape of the surrounding Marchfeld area of Vienna is not strictly delineated. The open space flows evenly through the residential complex and forms a tranquil, sunlit playground which benefits the existing houses as well.

PLAN

The apartments – oriented to the south and the west – are contained in four-storey wings, many with their own large loggia that provides private space. To retain the scale of the surrounding buildings, the architects refrained from building an additional rooftop level. The circulation typology is surprisingly rich in texture: two apartment wings are placed at differing angles, whereas one wing in each has a central feeder corridor. The third building, on the north edge, is an elongated block containing duplex apartments. The entrances connect the courtyard to all sides of the plot. All three upper floors are built from large prefabricated, laminated timber sections, while the basement is built in concrete and brick. The vertical loads are carried by the insulated partition walls between the apartments and the interior walls. Sound-absorbing floor plates act as continuous beams and extend above the transverse walls, their underside forming the finished ceilings.

The longitudinal facades, which are broken by numerous openings, are constructed from highly insulated framed panels, clad on the inside with plasterboard and on the outside with rear-ventilated, larch weatherboarding. The untreated facades are the external expression of the pure wooden structure of the building, and are combined with coloured shutters. Due to the flush-mounted surfaces, the timber facades will weather evenly, turn grey and, together with the shutters and loggias, offer an even more intense play of colours.

In order to meet the required fire safety standards, fire tests were conducted using prototypes of the timber facades. Instead of using expensive hardwoods, through the use of a 15 cm fire protective overhang between floors, it was possible to achieve the requisite fire rating using larch. These horizontal, wooden string courses are clad in sheet metal and serve as both the supports and guides for the sliding shutters. The wooden clad-

ding on the sides of the loggias is not carried around the corner to cover the external surfaces of the walls, as experience has shown the weathering of such details produces extreme contrasts on the exterior surfaces. Another novelty is the use of weatherproofed, prefabricated laminated timber elements in order to ensure the quality of construction on the site. The exterior access balconies are steel structures positioned in front of the main timber structure. They are equipped with non-flammable decks, made of precast concrete.

The projected heating energy consumption of 36 kWh/m^2/a conforms to energy efficiency guidelines. About half of the hot water is produced using a solar heating system. The generated energy savings correspond to the heating energy consumption of nine highly-insulated single-family houses.

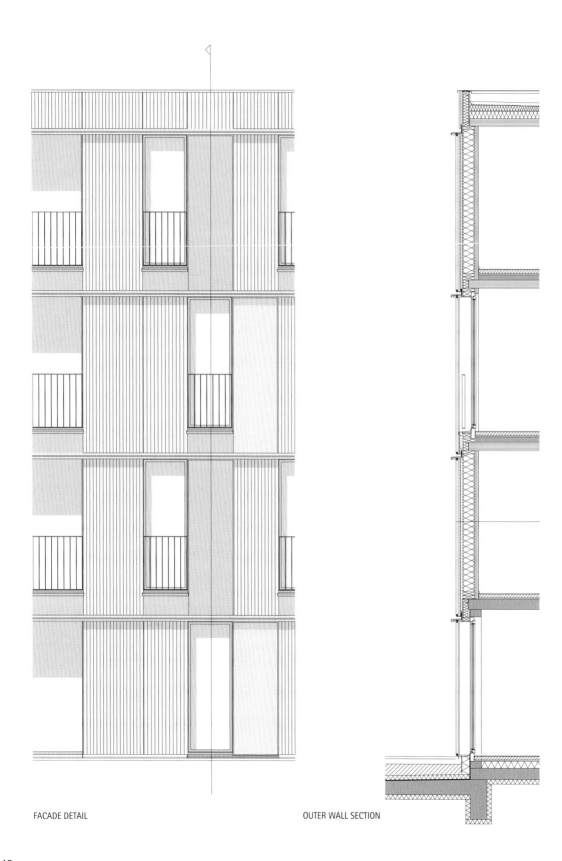

FACADE DETAIL

OUTER WALL SECTION

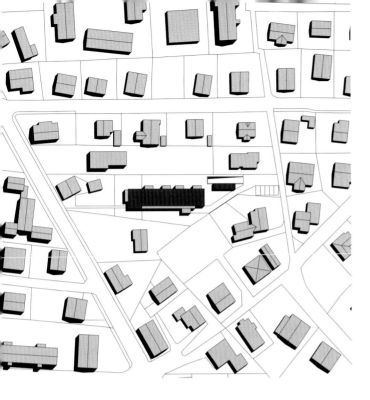

ÖLZBÜNDT
HOUSING ESTATE
Dornbirn, Vorarlberg, Austria, 1997
Text: Walter Zschokke

Ölzbündt, from the old German word *biunt*(a), is a word used in southern Germany, Switzerland and the Vorarlberg federal state in Austria for a vegetable garden that is fenced-in close to a house in order to protect it from wild animals. The long building structure of the Ölzbündt apartment block lies on a narrow plot within a zone of single-family houses on the north-eastern outskirts of the city of Dornbirn in Vorarlberg. The elongated three-storey building is clad with larch weatherboarding that emphasizes the volume of the structure. The balconies on the west side and the access walkways on the east side are built from slender steel members and with timber plank flooring. Hence the main structure and adjacent exterior spaces can be clearly differentiated. The stair tower forms the third structural element. Its individuality is emphasised by its glazed facades that project out from the main body of the building. The southern end of the block is taken up by a single-family residential unit integrated into the volume. An element of exterior space was added to the building in the form of the multi-level balconies. In the interior, the residential floors are both protected against fire and acoustically insulated by means of a concrete wall. The twelve apartments are compactly organized. Each of the units comprises either two or three rooms and all of them include a large room for the kitchen, dining and living area which extends the full depth of the building frame. The narrow tall windows with their deep reveals and the almost 0.5 metre-thick external walls give the building a massive feeling, despite the cost-efficient construction method used. The use of timber in the construction was not for provisional purposes, but rather is meant to achieve a sustainable use. The larch weatherboarding on the facades is protected by deep roof eaves, thus prolonging its life span without the need for protective wood treatments. Access to the

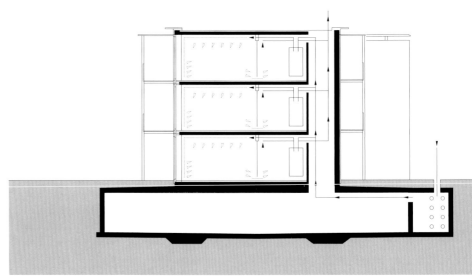

HEATING AND VENTILATION

underground parking garage and stairs is from the north side. However, there is a path leading from the wood-lined sheltered walkway on the north side via a stairs and bridge to the south side. On this side, too, the building is closely linked with its surroundings.

The three-storey, integral timber structure, based on a 2.4-metre grid, is primarily built from wood components that were manufactured as prefabricated elements by a carpentry workshop. This allowed for rapid assembly on site. Bonded timber panels, three-layer panels, plywood and solid timber planking were all used in accordance with their structural characteristics, weather resilience as well as design criteria. Economic considerations also played a major role in these decisions. The hollow, box-shaped roof elements were filled with gravel for sound insulation, and plasterboard panels were used in the interior.

Standard heating elements were not necessary due to the good heat-insulating properties of the exterior walls. No more then 26 kWh/m^2 per year are necessary since the building includes individually adjustable ventilation and heat exchangers and uses residual energy efficiently. Solar panels on the roof provide adequate warm water.

The energy concept makes use of the very well insulated, sealed and "thermal bridge free" building shell, making it possible to heat incoming air even if only a minimal amount of air is circulated. Compact, individually adjustable devices control the ventilation and heating in each apartment. Fresh air is heated to a minimum of 0° centigrade by a geothermal heat exchanger in each dwelling. Up to 60 per cent of the residual heat can be recycled via a plate heat exchanger. A small heat pump increases the incoming air temperature to a maximum of 40° centigrade. However, it is still possible to gain additional ventilation via the windows.

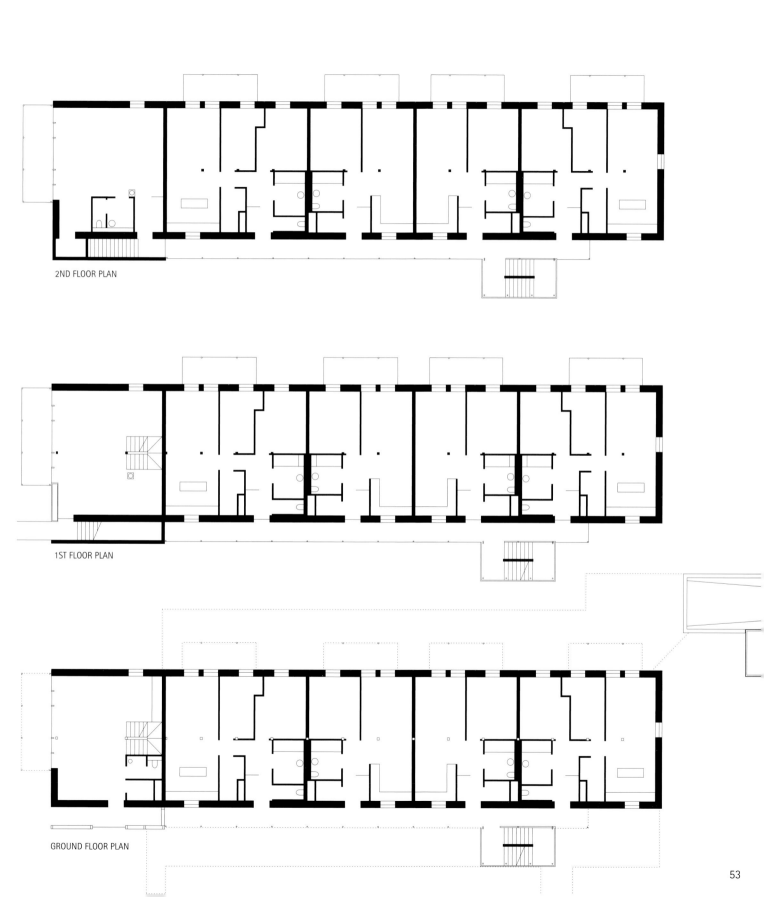

2ND FLOOR PLAN

1ST FLOOR PLAN

GROUND FLOOR PLAN

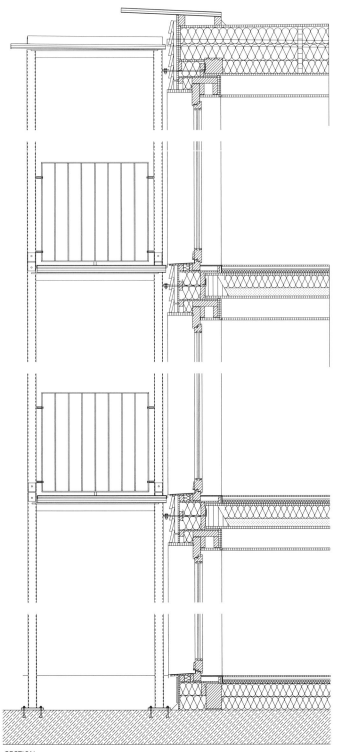

SECTION

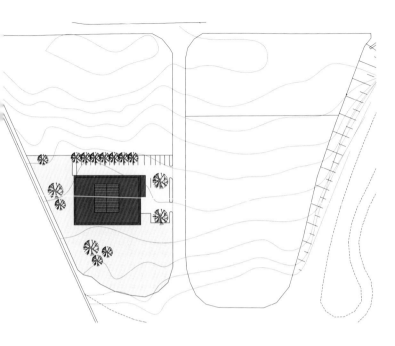

MM IMMOBILIEN ST. GEORGEN GMBH OFFICES

St. Georgen, Attergau, Austria, 2008
Text: Otto Kapfinger

St. Georgen, Attergau, the headquarters of a wood processing enterprise – with offices in Austria, Switzerland and Germany – features a novel, extremely economical, flexible construction made of spruce glulam from the company's own production. The building was designed using only a minimum of different materials, while employing an optimal amount of solid wood elements. The objective was to build a very simple structure with a minimal wall assembly, while maximizing the heat-storage capacity of the wooden structure and improving the spatial and functional qualities of the building. The cantilevered two-storey main structure sits atop a concrete base. A structural module of 2.58 m was used to meet both constructional and functional needs. In the interior the glulam wood supports are dimensioned according to this module, while 86 cm-wide slab-type glulam supports (one-third of the structural module) with wood-fibre insulation were placed along the exterior walls. Glulam wood beams rest atop the structure, carrying 86 cm-wide laminated wood ceiling elements that span the double unit spacing.

The conference room on the main level is column-free. The mono-pitched roof of the central, two-storey atrium incorporates glulam ridges which are only 8 cm wide and up to 1.80 m long. The archaic and simple architecture consists of large-scale volumes with homogenous wooden finishes and which are "cloaked" in cross-laminated timber canopies and balconies, mounted with steel strips within the structural module. This exterior layer forms a protective barrier against external noise; it carries mobile solar shading elements, and protects the untreated wood façade, while letting the users step outside from every room in the building.

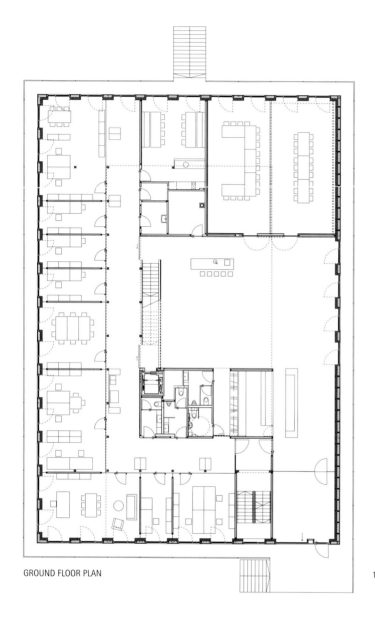

GROUND FLOOR PLAN

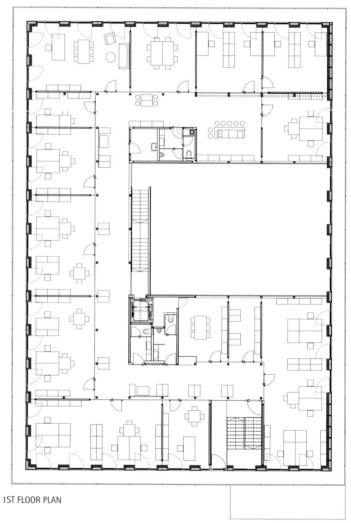

1ST FLOOR PLAN

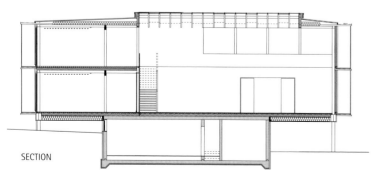

SECTION

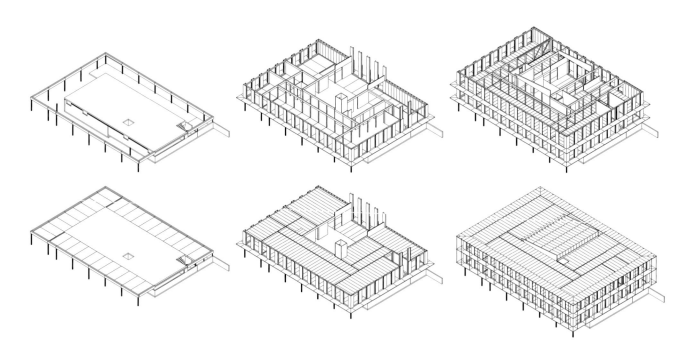

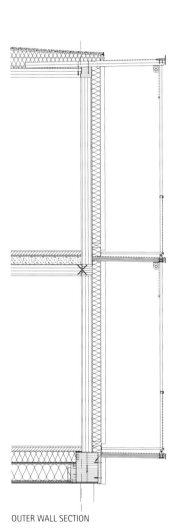

OUTER WALL SECTION

OFFICE AND RESIDENTIAL BUILDING SPORTPLATZWEG

Schwarzach, Vorarlberg, Austria, 1999
Cooperation with Christian Lenz
Text: Walter Zshokke

The oblong building is situated at the north end of the village where the settlement turns into sports fields and gardens.

The building is a similar height as the nearby single-family houses, but is clearly longer. The ground floor is mostly taken up by an open plan office. Connected directly to it are a few small rooms and a conference room which is buffered from surrounding sounds and direct views into it. The acoustics of the interior are improved by prefabricated wood-fibre elements suspended from the concrete intermediate floor. The floor is made from varnished chipboard.

On the upper floor are four flats with southward-facing terraces. The residential floor is wider than the ground floor, so its long facades create on both sides a canopy that protects the office windows below. Projecting out from the building, though integrated into the building frame, are two wooden staircase blocks, the facades of which are covered with a dark plastic fabric. The facades of the upper storey are covered with Douglas fir plywood. Each of the four flats is unique, spacious and well-functioning. The glulam roof beams give the living spaces a beautiful appearance and improve the acoustics. The layouts of the flats were determined by the functions: the bathroom, kitchen and toilet face north, whereas the dining room, living room and bedrooms face south. The spacious terrace increases the available living space. Later it would be possible to alter the room division of the flats without any structural problems. This flexibility is also implementable in the office floor. The use of lightweight dividing walls enables alterations, which is an important aspect in sustainable building.

Both the office and the flats are supplied with monitored air-conditioning and the additional energy required for heating comes from a gas boiler.

The air-conditioning and heating function as follows: the outside air is brought in through a duct supplied with a prefilter, along sealed plastic pipes situated approximately one metre below the basement floor. The central ground-air heat exchanger heats the air in winter and cools it in summer. The intake air quality is improved by natural air ionisation.

Every flat has its own independently controlled air conditioning unit, supplied with heat retention, fans, filters, air heater, microprocessor automation and remote control. The air conditioning unit changes the air in the room approximately 0.7 times per hour. The outside air entering the air conditioning unit is filtered one additional time and heated when necessary afterwards. The air flows into the room from an outlet in the ceiling or wall. The air flow is slow; in the living room less than 0.15 m/s. The air is extracted from the bathroom, toilet and kitchen through a disc valve. The doors between the rooms are not air tight so that air can flow via the corridor and entrance hall to the spaces where the extract vents are situated. In the small flats the extract vent is situated in the kitchen fan, which functions as an air-circulating fan. In the large flats the kitchen fan functions as the extract vent for the living spaces.

The bathrooms have underfloor heating. In the living rooms – the exterior walls of which have large areas of glass – there is also wall heating to provide additional warmth on cold days. There is basic heating in the each flat that is kept on continuously during the winter. The air flow can be adjusted so that it is slow during the night and faster during the daytime. The warm water for the flats and the office is produced by solar collectors installed on the terrace balustrade. In the wintertime additional energy is provided by natural gas.

In the office space the air is extracted through the ceiling and led back to the air conditioning unit and out via a heat exchanger. In the wintertime only the amount of air necessary for good air quality is exchanged and the rest is circulated back into the room via an ionizer. In the summertime all air is led through the ground-air heat exchanger for cooling purposes. All office rooms have a low-temperature radiant heating system under the window ledge. This produces pleasant convective heat and supports the flow of air in the room. Ventilation in the office can be regulated individually.

In terms of energy optimisation, the building requires high-quality insulation and detailed design of the building envelope. The ceiling of the basement is a well-insulated wood construction with studs that allow for easy access for any necessary maintenance. The ceiling of the ground floor, on the other hand, is built in concrete, which stores and disperses heat, and provides sound insulation between the office and residential floors. The floors of the flats are built from easily assembled wood boarding with 35 cm of insulation. The single-shell flat roof is constructed from narrow Douglas fir glulam beams, and with 40 cm of insulation. The plinth is covered with coloured OSB panels. The open stairwells are covered with a fabric. There was a conscious decision to experiment with different materials in the building.

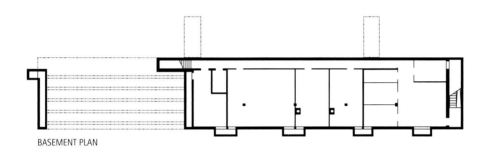

BASEMENT PLAN

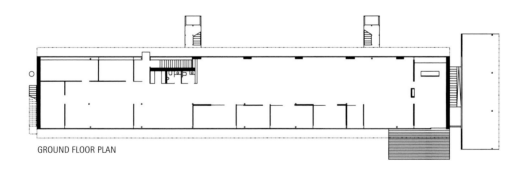

GROUND FLOOR PLAN

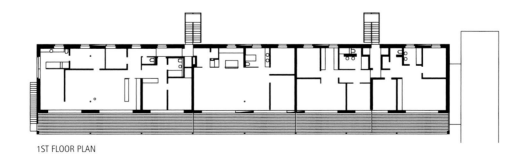

1ST FLOOR PLAN

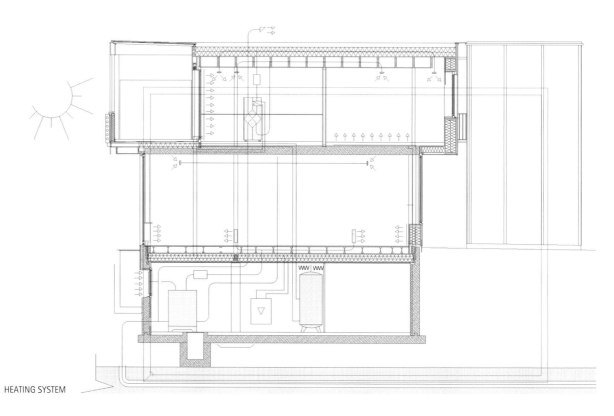

HEATING SYSTEM

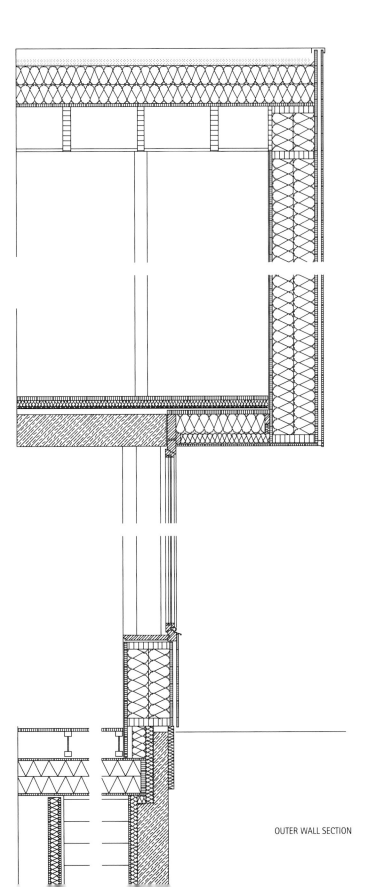

OUTER WALL SECTION

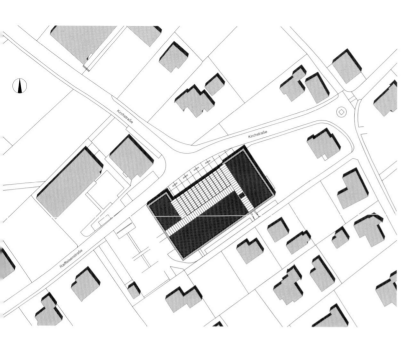

LUDESCH COMMUNITY CENTRE

Ludesch, Vorarlberg, Austria, 2005
Text: Otto Kapfinger

The community centre, first opened in 2005, is an exemplary building in Europe, and has received both national and international awards. Ludesch is a municipality in Vorarlberg, Austria, with approximately 3000 inhabitants. Ecological awareness has a long tradition there. In 1994, the local council decided to join the international Climate Alliance. In 1995, the energy efficiency of the local building fabric was assessed; based on this assessment, a program of locally funded energy incentives was launched in 1997. In 1998, Ludesch became a member of Vorarlberg's "e5-Program", which is a province-wide initiative for the qualification and certification of energy-efficient municipalities.

The need for a new community centre had already been determined in 1995. A workgroup was established in 1998, and in 2000 Hermann Kaufmann's office was initially integrated into the process and then finally commissioned with the planning. The aim was to establish a community centre as an ecological prototype – at a reasonable cost and with participation from the local residents in the development process.

The small scale and heterogeneity of the recently grown linear village necessitated a re-interpretation of the spatial situation of its central area. On account of the village's diffuse agglomeration, neither a concentrated centre nor a traditional village square had existed. The spatial interrelation of the church, school and old municipal offices was rather incoherent. The new two-storey building, built opposite the old un-renovated municipal offices, presents itself as an urban "bracket", framing a courtyard that opens to the northwest, towards the arrival point from the village road.

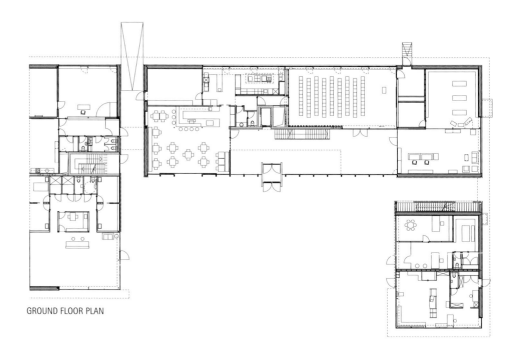

GROUND FLOOR PLAN

The planning and construction were an interdisciplinary effort. The team included officials of the municipal government, the Environmental Association of Voralberg and the Austrian Institute for Healthy and Ecological Building (IBO), as well as Hermann Kaufmann Architects and a consultant in charge of quality assurance on the construction site. Tenders were invited for both conventional and green building methods. In the end, a green building was executed – at an additional cost of only 1.9 %.

The three volumes of the community centre enclose and define a forecourt. Each wing is assigned a specific function: the ground level contains a post office, shop, large foyer, library, café, 100-person capacity hall, physiotherapy practice and day nursery; the upper floor contains offices, seminar rooms, archives, computer centre and public toilets; the basement – with its adjoining rooms, rehearsal and club rooms – connects the various wings of the complex. Both roof levels feature cantilevered stringcourses which protect the natural wood facades and the large format doors and glazing from rain and harsh weather generally. Below these bitumen-clad timber slabs are adjustable, cable-mounted solar screens that shade the window areas. The lightly sloping terrain allows for skylights on the southeast side of the basement, thus providing daylight to the club rooms situated there. The universal application of silver fir – used on all surfaces, from walls to furniture – unifies the manifold functions into a harmonious indoor atmosphere that wins people over with its visual, acoustic and sensual qualities.

A two-storey timber construction was erected over a reinforced concrete basement. The walls and ceilings are prefabricated box beams; the facades as well as the interior walls and ceilings are clad in silver fir. Depending on its particular use, the cladding is rough-sawn, wire-brushed or smoothly planed; the flooring of dark-oiled oak is the contrasting element in the composition. The timber used for the structure and the facade was grown locally. The exterior walls were insulated with cellulose, while sheep wool was used as insulation material for the fit-out and finishes.

Sheep wool also replaced the commonly used polyurethane window insulation. Solid walls stiffen the structure, while slender steel columns were integrated into the structure where slimmer profiles were desired. The selection of building materials served to promote the following criteria: promotion of regional economic activity; usage of native wood; protection of exterior wood surfaces by architectural means – no wood coatings; insulation made from renewable resources; non-use of PVC, solvents or materials that contain formaldehydes and halogenated fluorocarbon.

The constructive wooden elements were prefabricated in the production halls of two local companies and assembled on site. Concrete anchors, screws and adhesive tape were used for assembly in place of glued connections. Meticulous attention was paid to the sealing of the construction as well as to avoiding the use of substances that could – both during construction and after completion – negatively impact the healthiness of the indoor environment.

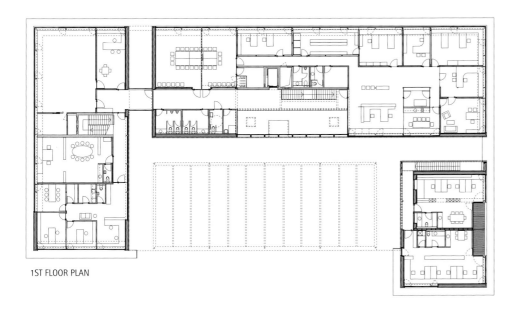

1ST FLOOR PLAN

In addition to the calculable thermal optimization, the project in Ludesch also aimed at reducing the primary energy consumption of the construction process ("invested energy") by 50 % compared to "standard" passive buildings. It was further intended to halve the ecological footprint of the building envelope compared to conventional architecture. The goal was to achieve a passive house standard with a heating energy consumption rate of 15 kWh/m²/a. The projected heating energy use of 13.8 kWh/m²/a is extremely low and was accomplished by the following means: excellent thermal insulation for heat protection, well-sealed building envelope, and a state-of-the-art ventilation system with heat recovery. The ventilation system is connected to a groundwater pump and supplies the rooms – according to their specific uses – with pre-heated or pre-cooled fresh air. In winter the groundwater temperature is used to generate heat and in summer to generate cooling. Air humidity inside the building is constantly monitored and adjusted. Hot water is generated through solar panels on the roof – covering a total area of 30m². Additional heat energy is supplied by the biomass district heating plant. While the built volume of the community centre equals that of approximately 22 single family homes, it only uses as much energy for heating or cooling as two conventional detached houses. The supply air is tempered to a maximum of 22 °C. The humidifier is integrated into the ventilation unit. All mechanical systems are outfitted with meters, to allow computer-based monitoring of energy use.

Early in the planning, the municipality decided to roof over the new town square to allow for a variety of uses. After conducting several preliminary studies, an innovative, environmentally friendly and polyvalent solution was found. The translucent photovoltaic panels – with a surface area of 350 m² – are not just a mere weather-protective design twist for the covered square, the wooden facade and the windows. They also generate 16,000 kWh of electricity each year. The power generated is fed into the grid of the Vorarlberger Kraftwerke (regional power plant) and supplies electricity to five households.

To maximize the efficiency of the photovoltaic unit, the different zones are interconnected – essentially, all top cells and middle cells of a zone are wired together. To ensure maximum transparency of the glass roof, the photovoltaic cells feature a grid of 5 x 5 mm openings. As a result, the forecourt receives an ideal amount of shade, without being too dark. This state-of-the-art system, which was specifically developed for Ludesch, is expected to generate approximately 320,000 kWh of electricity over the next 20 years.

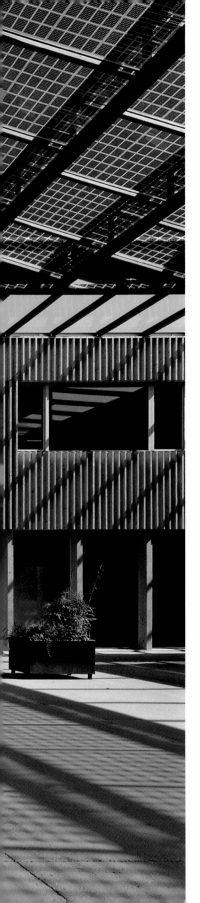

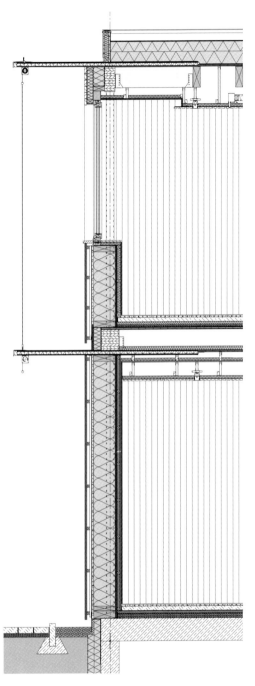

OUTER WALL SECTION

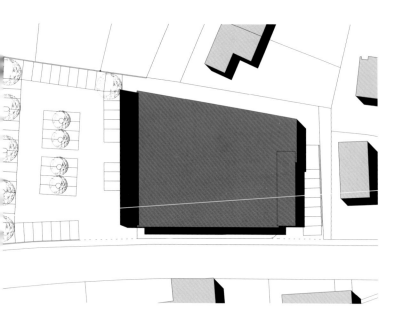

SUTTERLÜTY
SUPERMARKET

Weiler, Vorarlberg, Austria, 2002
Text: Otto Kapfinger

This regional supermarket chain, already well established in Vorarlberg, is opening a series of new stores that break new ground both in terms of goods offered and the type of spatial organization: the common ailes of shelves have been replaced by clearly arranged square-like spaces with a coffee bar and farmer's-market-like stalls that offer fresh local products, all of which has been successfully integrated into the local context. Sutterlüty was searching for a spatial structure and a material concept that provides optimum flexibility and allows for variations, using only a few elements; in short, for a method of construction that is both economical and sustainable and that provides a strong framework and background for the "visual presentation" of the goods.

For the interior of the building in Weiler, Hermann Kaufmann designed a special timber ceiling construction above the main sales space – the dominant surface in the space – which acts as the "background" that determines the interior atmosphere. The 47 cm thick roof slab, with a surface area of 1500 m², covers the interior space at a height of 5 m as well as the exterior space – with projections on the north (entrance) and south sides (delivery). The roof slab consists of spruce hollow-core elements that are placed between the outer walls and the main girders made of cross-laminated timber, which also carry the load of the interior space via two-hinged steel bars. The hollow core elements span 14 m; the 1.85 m wide prefabricated elements are clad with three-layer slabs on both sides, the lower slab constituting the finished ceiling.

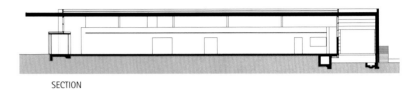

SECTION

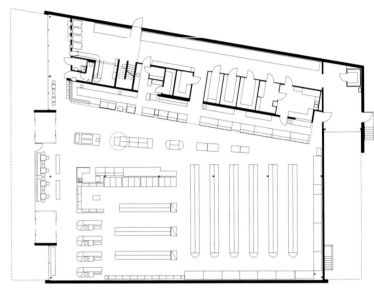

GROUND FLOOR PLAN

In order to maintain the homogeneity of the bright spruce ceiling, the main girders, which have a width of up to 72 cm, have also been integrated into the ceiling. For installation purposes, a few lower sheathing strips were omitted and closed with three-layer slabs after completion of the pipe work. The lighting is suspended from the ceiling and directed into the sales area. In addition to quick assembly, the specific material properties of the timber roof slab also prevent the formation of a thermal bridge, and allow a smooth transition of the slab through the glazed front facade into the projections of the canopies. This (by its sheer visual appearance "monolithic") roof slab also has a structural function, namely to brace the building.

The longitudinal side walls consist of timber-frame constructions that are clad with oriented strand boarding (colour coordinated with the red floor) and with an outer layer of vapour-permeable composite wood boards. The exterior wall cladding of the closed west facade, which faces the road, is made of vertically mounted acacia boarding that displays the subtle "random texture" of the different formats available from the factory.

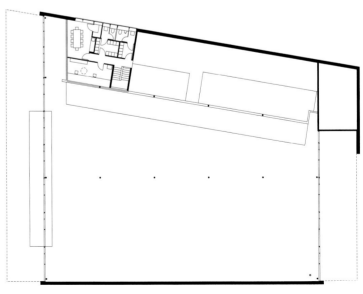

1ST FLOOR PLAN

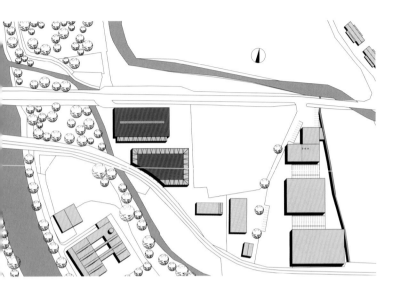

METZLER TIMBER WAREHOUSE AND OFFICES

Bezau, Vorarlberg, Austria, 1995
Text: Hermann Kaufmann Office

Metzler is a company, with premises in Bezau and Schwarzach, that specialises in supplying sawn and planed timber. It is a traditional family enterprise and is known for its high-class products for both domestic and foreign markets. 90 % of its products are exported, and approximately 95% of the logs come from forests in the region. The company mainly produces wood for the manufacture of windows but also for other professional use in the building industry. It also sells dried sawn timber directly to companies in the crafts industry that do not have their own storage facilties. Thus the construction of the warehouse with a capacity for storing approximately 3000 m^3 of wood fulfills a real need. Naturally the main building material for the warehouse for timber was wood. In the construction it was important to take into consideration that the main building material would be solid wood, the span of the space would be 30 metres, and the roof would take a snow load of 400 kg/m^2. Accordingly, the main bearing structure was designed as a lenticular truss, the upper arch and diagonal infills of which are solid wood whereas the lower arch is curved glulam.

The roof structure rests on steel columns. The facades were constructed from prefabricated elements that were fastened to the steel columns. The elements consist of a solid wood frame clad with coarse-sawn spruce planks. On top of the lenticular trusses, which are spaced at a distance of 5 metres, are solid wood roof purlins and 30 mm thick roof boarding.

A particular novelty of the building is the wide cantilevered awning fixed to the exterior wall. It is built using the so-called Brettstapelbau technique whereby parallel planks are fixed to form plane elements, and which in this case are fastened to the building with steel rods. The same technique has also been used for the ceilings of the two-storey office section built

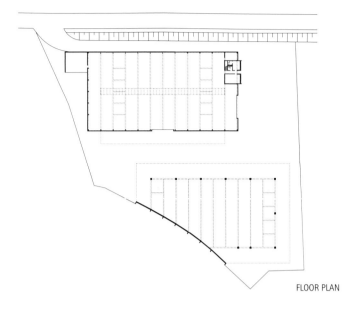

FLOOR PLAN

inside the warehouse, the walls of which are based on a timber-frame construction.

To put such a building volume in the beautiful scenery of Bregenzerwald requires courage and a sense of aesthetics. An important factor is, of course, the choice of material for the building. Wood is indeed a traditional building material acquired from the surrounding district, the properties of which are well suited and adapt with time to the surroundings.

The upper part of the building is a glass construction that prevents the 12-metre high warehouse space from appearing too tall. The top of the building appears to dissolve, appearing lightweight and transparent and illuminating the interior. "The eaves and gutter beneath the window lists provde the fine details that complement the overall robust impression and make the difference between structural architecure and mere engineering skill " (Otto Kapfinger).

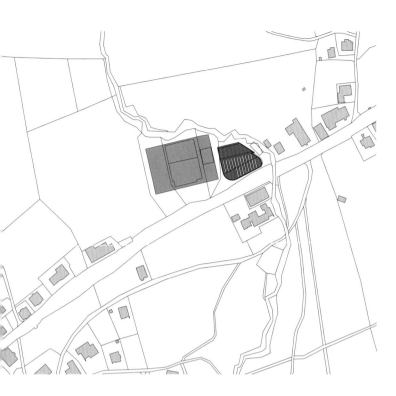

SOHM HOLZBAU OFFICE AND INDUSTRIAL BUILDING, EXTENSION

Alberschwende, Vorarlberg, Austria, 2009
Text: Hermann Kaufmann Office

Sohm, an innovative and successful company in Alberschwende, Bregenzerwald, that specialises in wood construction, expanded its operations by acquiring an additional site. The steeply sloping site allowed the construction of storage space and a new heating system in a basement floor, above which is a roofed but partly open multi-purpose hall on the ground floor and a two-storey office section. The challenge was to fit the building on the uneven plot and link together architectonically the large open multi-purpose work hall and the small office section.

The exterior envelope, built from vertically placed wood lamellas and plexiglass, creates a pleasant totality that is adapted precisely to the shape of the plot. The rounded corners strengthen the external envelope. The office section, which is constructed completely from wood, rests on a massive basement floor, above which is the roof of the open work hall.

Sohm manufactures solid wood elements that are not joined together with glue, but rather with joined together with beech dowels drilled at an angle. The office section was built completely from these elements, which defines the appearance of the interior. The untreated glue-free timber ensures a healthy working environment. This is an example of modern wood construction that represents the technological development of our time, and which through its innovative properties renews the tradition of solid wood construction.

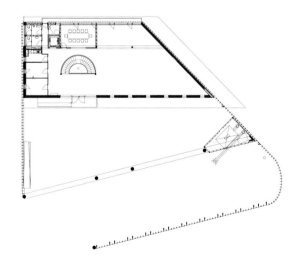

GROUND FLOOR PLAN

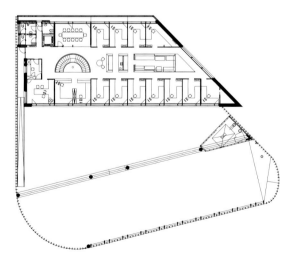

1ST FLOOR PLAN

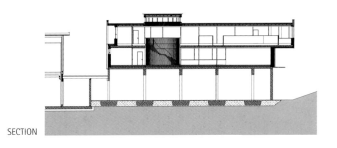

SECTION

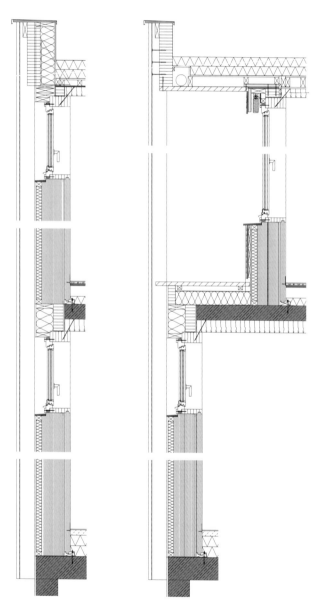

DETAILS OF THE EXTERIOR WALL

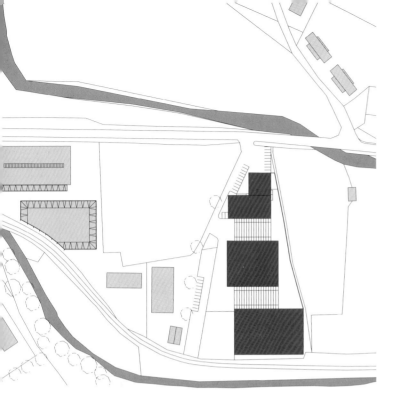

WÄLDERHAUS INDUSTRIAL PARK

Bezau, Vorarlberg, Austria, 2002
Text: Otto Kapfinger

Industrial and commercial parks are few and far between in this region, whose main source of revenue is agriculture. The design of new buildings is often left to chance, despite their impact on the natural landscape. This project on the periphery of Bezau benefitted from a previous intervention by Kaufmann, who had built the timber production halls in close vicinity to the new wooden structure of the Wälderhaus industrial park; what results from the two industrial complexes is a sort of timber city. The aim of the design was to integrate the new volumes into the landscape using balanced forms and natural wood. Similar to the existing buildings, typical features of the new structure include the strip windows below the eaves and the wooden envelope extending almost all the way to the floor. The warehouses, production halls, metalworking shop and offices are knitted into the large building, marked out only by the window openings in the facade. One L- and two square-shaped halls use a staggered arrangement in response to the shape of the plot. The halls are connected by vaulted roofs, partially glazed and built of steel to meet fire protection requirements. The vaulted roofs span between the building masses, without over-exaggerating the dimensions of the composition. As a result of the terrain, from the village the industrial park appears even lower, leaving the view of the landscape below the vaulted roofs unobstructed.

SECTION

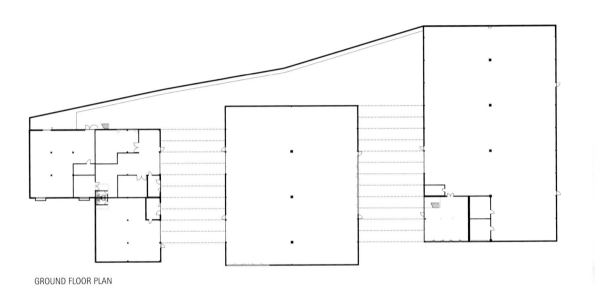

GROUND FLOOR PLAN

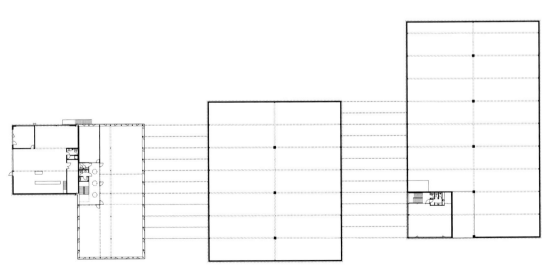

1ST FLOOR PLAN

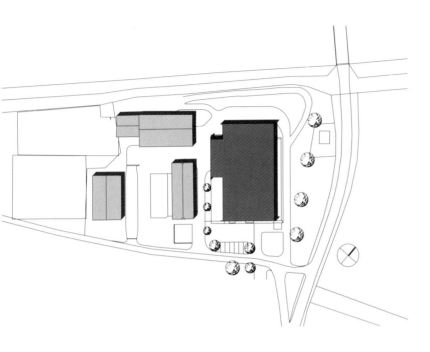

RHEINHOF ESTATE

Hohenems, Vorarlberg, Austria, 2006

Text: Otto Kapfinger

The barn for 110 animals is part of the organically farmed teaching premises of the agricultural college in Hohenems. Together with school representatives, local farmers and agriculture officials, Hermann Kaufmann developed an efficient alternative to conventional barns with a pitched roof. To allow light and air into the 46 m long and 30 m wide barn, the building envelope takes the shape – in section – of a basilica. The pitched roof directs light into the building though vertical skylights, while providing a natural chimney effect to circulate the air. The longitudinal elevations feature unglazed window bands under a protective eaves. Translucent blinds can be lowered to protect these openings against strong wind and rain.

The entire structure is built of solid timber grown locally; a new joining method is used to hold together the frame, replacing traditional glulam wood. The structural system's appearance is airy and marked by a large number of individual elements. This is related to the decision to use timber from nearby forests: the length of the wood was limited to that which could be acquired locally. Glulam technology was not used due to its environmental impact. Thus, together with structural engineer and carpenter Konrad Merz, Kaufmann developed adequate frame elements by creating double and triple layers of jointed solid wood beams. The details are simple and the joints require only a small number of steel elements. Threaded metal rods carry the tension loads; their slenderness contributes to the building's light and airy appearance. The central nave consists of pitched trusses, while the aisles are supported by simple beams. Beams made of plain-sawn wood are placed on top of the primary support structure. The exterior walls were prefabricated and feature vertical cladding and open joints, allowing air to enter without creating a draft.

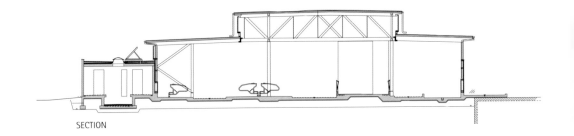

SECTION

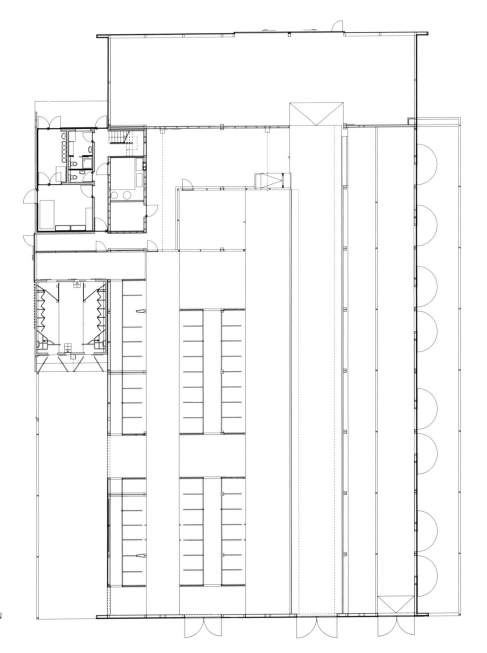

FLOOR PLAN

An office perches like a pulpit above the space, affording a view of the entire barn. In contrast to conventional barns with prefabricated metal doors that often seem collaged on to the building, here the doors have also been made of wood, in keeping with the theme of the building: altogether an exemplary teaching farm whose design has set new standards for high-quality agricultural buildings.

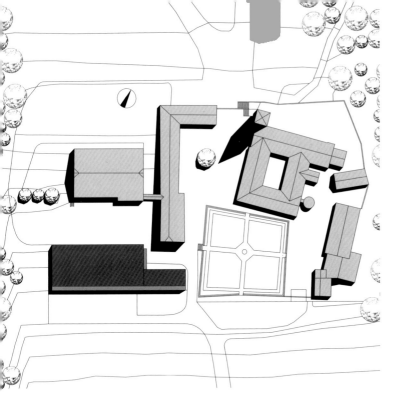

ST. GEROLD RIDING HALL

St. Gerold, Vorarlberg, Austria, 1997

Text: Walter Zschokke

After decades of decay, the St. Gerold provostry was carefully restored and now serves as a supra-regional cultural centre. The building complex is located on a sunny site on the south side of the mountain facing the Großer Walsertal Valley. After the renovation of the existing facilities, it was decided to expand the complex to include a riding hall for disabled and paraplegic patient therapy. The building also includes facilities for a small Haflinger horse-breeding facility. The new building extends from the south-western corner of the convent building, framing a garden-courtyard space. At the same time, its alignment parallel to the slope and barn on the opposite side of the yard helps delineate the farming section of the complex. The large mono-pitched roof extending over the entire building follows the general incline of the slope.

The interior of the riding hall is characterised by a sense of protected openness due to the commanding presence of the roof and the large areas of glass on three sides. The visitor does not feel that he is in an enclosed space. This is due to the fact that the space is not centred on a single axis, but instead strives to push outwards, due to the mono-pitched roof construction and the views towards the surrounding trees. On the south side there are large sliding doors which open out to a fenced area where the horses can be exercised or graze. The broad, projecting roof canopy includes a skylight that provides the riding hall with ample natural light, especially during the wintertime. The slender vertical struts also act as supports for the window wall construction. Single-glazed windows were used since they allow for greater transparency and less reflection than the more commonly used double-glazed windows. Hence the riding hall offers protection from wind and inclement weather, but retains the feeling of an open patch of land. Insulation was not required since the sun regulates the interior temperature.

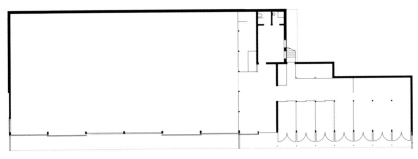

GROUND FLOOR PLAN

The roof construction consists of timber struts between which the roofing boards are visible, further supported in the middle by a row of splayed trusses each made up of six struts. The converging, pyramid-shaped trusses rest on the tips of steel tension bars. The black, slender steel tension bars seem to fade into the background, hence the trusses seem paradoxically to hover above the space, giving it an unorthodox sense of dynamism. The diagonal structural elements set on the interior side of the glass walls to provide support against the wind, are similarly unpretentious since they are almost invisible in back-lit conditions. Thus timber and steel are used according to their potential and with clear architectural intentions.

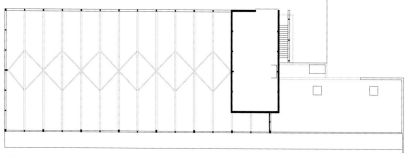

1ST FLOOR PLAN

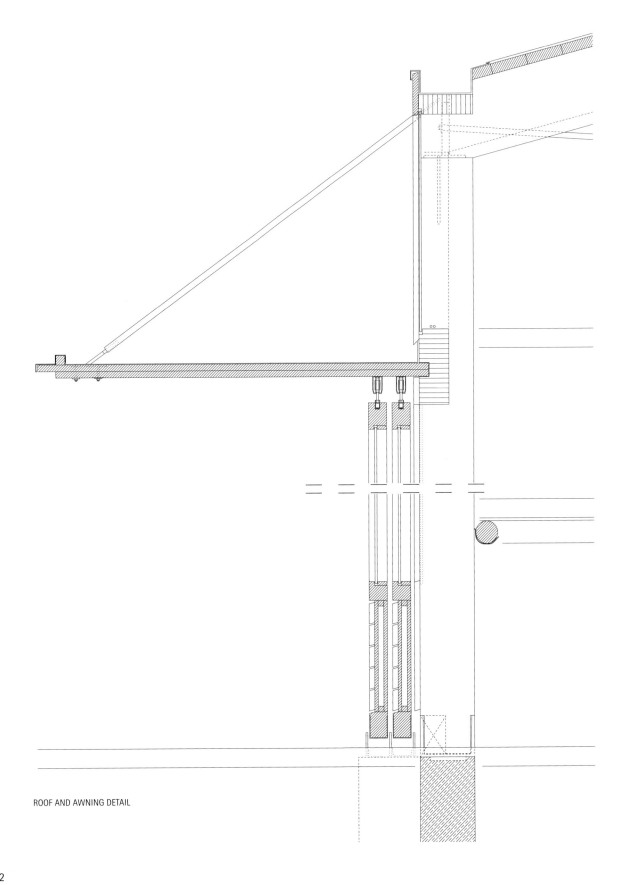

ROOF AND AWNING DETAIL

115

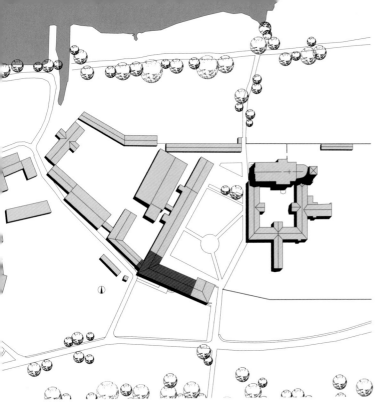

MEHRERAU GYMNASIUM, CONVERSION

Mehrerau, Bregenz, Vorarlberg, Austria, 1997
Cooperation with Christian Lenz
Text: Walter Zschokke

The old monastery lies on the eastern edge of the deltas that were created over the course of millennia by Bregenz's Ach. The crystalline appearance of the centre of the expansive complex, which consists of the church, cloister and modular wing, is framed by a large angular building structure at the western end of the complex built at an angle to the centre, hence creating a broad, open courtyard. The north-western end of the complex is marked by former commercial buildings. Many of the wings in the complex had been used for centuries for educational purposes, but were no longer adequate for changing needs. It was therefore necessary to replace the dilapidated segment on the southern side of the complex and replace it with suitable new classrooms. With its double-pitched roof, the new structure melds with the existing buildings. The masonry base course of the building, with its partially flat cross-vaulting, stretches from one neighbouring wing to the other, framing the new annex in the manner of a bracket. In constructing the annex, due to weight considerations on what was regarded as a challenging construction site, the space between the wings was filled by a timber construction with a large glazed façade. Architecturally, the new annex is the central element of the facility on "open display". The dynamic asymmetry of the façade remains more or less focused on the centre, despite the attractive adjacent masonry gable. The box-like classroom block projects out slightly from the base. It is separated from the existing wall structure by glazed walls with slender mullions. Immediately behind the glazed walls are small carrel-like niches, where people can stand contemplating their thoughts. Natural light enters into the central hallway from the north side. The vertical access, stairs and lift are placed to the east of the vaulted entrance hall. These were placed so as not to be seen from the outside since it would have detracted from the

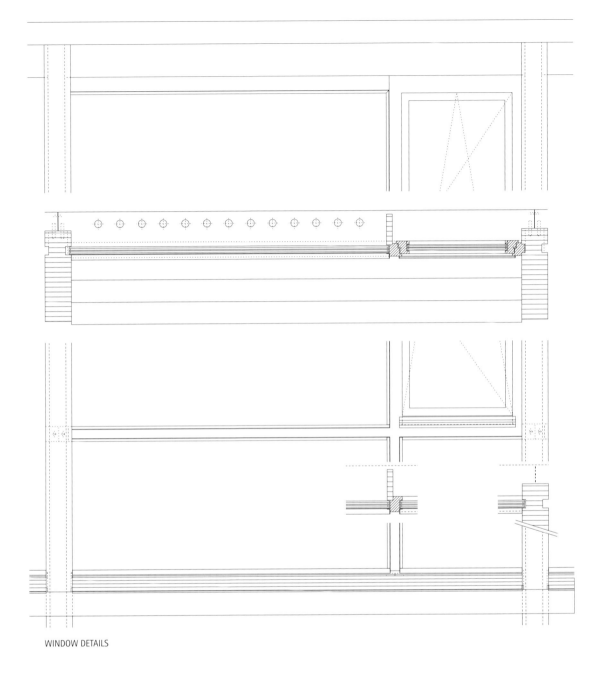

WINDOW DETAILS

calm lines of the façade. The regular rhythm of the new window subdivision follows the historical subdivision of the building and corresponds to the width of the interior vaulting. This helps maintain the proportions of the complex, despite the use of alternative materials and light construction techniques, as opposed to solid walls.

The primary bonded wooden structure comprises a frame of vertical struts and horizontal beams that connects to the roof's robust hollow box elements. The space projects outward towards the north and the stress is absorbed by the slender steel struts along the base wall. The roof covers the entire depth of the wing, with steel beams supporting the hollow box roof. The steel beams converge with the concrete walls of the classrooms, which act as storage space. The façade struts are spruce timber with a thick additional layer of ash wood. This is not only for exterior protection, but also helps define the character of the entire complex. Large glass panels were mounted directly within the façade frame if they were not intended as openable windows. Thus the support structures, struts and glass panes define the overall image. A monitored ventilation system supplies the classrooms with fresh air via the hollow roof channels.

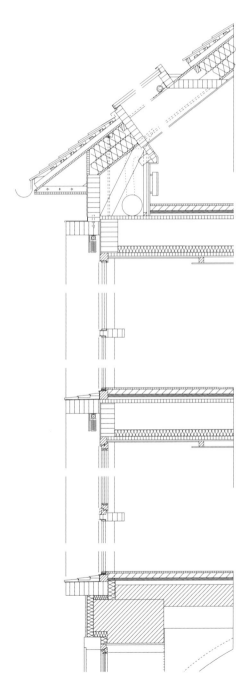

OUTER WALL SECTION

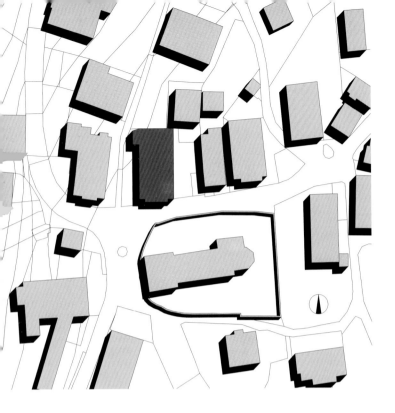

ADLER INN, RENOVATION

Schwarzenberg, Vorarlberg, Austria, 1991
Text: Hermann Kaufmann Office

Schwarzenberg is a village in the district of Bregenzerwald, Austria. In the village there are unusually many well-preserved historical buildings. In particular, the village centre is known as a typical Bregenzerwaldian village square. The square is bordered by the church, dance hall, as well as the Schäfle, Hirschen, Adler and Ochsen inns. The Schäfle and Ochsen inns are no longer operating, whereas the Hirschen and Adler inns have become increasingly popular. The Adler Inn was built in 1756. During reparations in 1865 the angle of the roof was made steeper and clad in shingles. It was repaired and renewed several times in the 1960s and 1970s, as a result of which a lot of the old structure was destroyed.

In 1985 Engelbert Kaufmann rented the inn and managed, despite the bad state of the building, to turn it into a good quality restaurant. In 1990 he bought the building and decided to have it completely renovated.

There was hardly anything in the building worth preserving, except for one guest room in the south-east corner. Consequently, it was possible to carry out new and unique ideas in both the floor plan and interior design. The central corridor on the ground floor was continued through the building, from which connections were opened to other spaces. A glass wall marks the central part of the corridor, where it widens and opens out towards a garden.

The guest rooms were renewed either in accordance with the original appearance or by adding simple waxed solid spruce panelling. The objective was to create a contemporary look through traditional handicraft methods without, however, losing the atmosphere typical for an old inn.

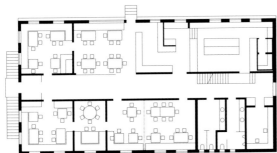

FLOOR PLAN

Surprisingly, when the exterior facades were renovated, the old main decorative facade was revealed. This was then renovated in cooperation with the building conservation authorities. Also the existing windows were replaced with wood-framed mullioned windows and hinged shutters following the original style.

The village of Schwarzenberg is now one historical building richer and the renewed inn has revived the "dead" village centre.

MESMERS STABLE, CONVERSION

Alberschwende, Vorarlberg, Austria, 2004
Cooperation with Dieter Seeberger
Text: Otto Kapfinger

Alberschwende is a municipality located at the threshold between the Bregenzerwald hills and the Rhine Valley; with a population of 3000, it is situated more than 700 metres above sea level. The characteristic village centre – church, town hall, country inn – is set amongst traditional farmsteads complete with barns and stables. However, as in most comparable villages of the region, most agricultural outbuildings lie in a state of disuse. Their preservation and reuse is, nevertheless, of crucial importance for the identity of the settlement structure.

The old stable in Alberschwende, located in the second row of the village centre, belonged to the estate of the so-called Mesmer house. The municipality and its mayor, Walter Rüf, decided to convert the building into a small agricultural museum which could double as an attractive venue for small events, meetings, concerts and festivities. In the course of the conversion, as much of the old building fabric was preserved as possible. Silver fir, a traditional local material, was used for the extensions and fittings, producing a sensitive dialogue between the clean, abstract details of the new intervention and the rough surfaces of the existing structure and which bear testimony to the craft tradition and to the harsh living conditions of the past. Two large skylights and a wide footbridge draw attention to the the building's new use.

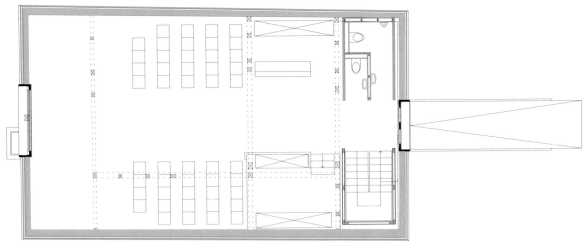

1ST FLOOR PLAN

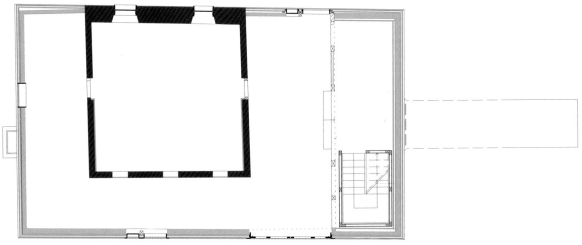

GROUND FLOOR PLAN

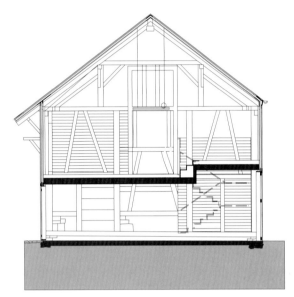

CROSS SECTION

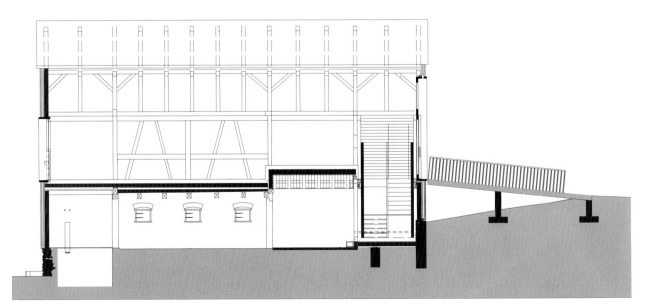

LONGITUDAL SECTION

project information

Building	Zerlauth House
Architect / chief designer	Hermann Kaufmann
Assistants	Juliane Wiljotti, Gerold Hämmerle, Norbert Kaufmann
Year of completion	2003
Floor area	181 m^2
Gross area	320 m^2
Volume	1.051 m^3
Location	Beim Feldgatter 4, A-6820 Frastanz, Vorarlberg, Austria
Client	Elisa and Markus Zerlauth
Specialist design	M+G Ingenieure, Josef Galehr, Reinhard Moser, Planungsbüro, Manuel Krekeler
Photographs	Bruno Klomfar

Building	Olperer Hut
Architect / chief designer	Hermann Kaufmann
Assistants	Claudia Greussing, Julia Nägele-Küng, Gerold Hämmerle
Construction period	2006–2007
Floor area	592 m^2
Gross area	677 m^2
Volume	2.174 m^3
Location	Ginzling, Zillertal, Tyrol, Austria
Client	DAV Deutscher Alpenverein
Specialist design	merz kley partner, Walter Ingenieure GmbH
Photographs	Hermann Kaufmann

Building	Bicycle Bridge
Architect / chief designer	Hermann Kaufmann
Assistants	Amt der Vorarlberger Landesregierung, Martin Rümmele
Year of construction	1999
Location	A-6974 Gaißau, Altes Zollamt, Vorarlberg, Austria
Client	Amt der Vorarlberger Landesregierung
Specialist design	DI Frank Dickbauer, Kurt Düngler
Photographs	Ignacio Martinez

Building	Elma Alp Vacation Home
Architect / chief designer	Hermann Kaufmann
Assistants	Christoph Dünser, Benjamin Baumgartl, Gerold Hämmerle, Norbert Kaufmann
Construction period	2004–2005
Floor area	175 m²
Gross area	172 m²
Volume	360 m³
Location	A-6881 Mellau, Austria
Client	Andreas Dorner
Specialist design	Mader & Flatz Ziviltechniker GmbH, Steurer Siegfried, Schneider Hubert
Photographs	Bruno Klomfar

Building	Mühlweg Housing Estate
Architect / chief designer	Hermann Kaufmann
Assistants	Christoph Dünser, Martin Rümmele
Construction period	2005–2006
Floor area	7.617 m²
Gross area	8.170 m²
Volume	23.755 m³
Location	Fritz-Kandl-Gasse 7, A-1020 Wien, Austria
Client	BWS Gemeinnützige Allgemeine Bau-, Wohn- und Siedlungsgen. Reg. Gen.m.b.H.
Specialist design	merz kaufmann partner GmbH, Pesek Planungsbüro, s.d. & engineering, Holzforschung Austria, PlanSinn GmbH
Photographs	Bruno Klomfar

Building	Ölzbundt Housing Estate
Architect / chief designer	Hermann Kaufmann
Assistants	Norbert Kaufmann, Wolfgang Elmenreich
Year of construction	1997
Floor area	1.900 m²
Gross area	2.300 m²
Volume	5.475 m³
Location	Hamerlingstraße 12, A-6850 Dornbirn, Vorarlberg, Austria
Client	Anton Kaufmann und Gerold Ölz
Specialist design	merz kaufmann partner GmbH, GMI Ingenieure, Hecht Elektroplanungsbüro, Lothar Künz ZT GmbH
Photographs	Ignacio Martinez

Building	MM Immobilien St. Georgen GmbH Offices
Architect / chief designer	Hermann Kaufmann
Assistants	Juliane Wiljotti, Roland Wehinger, Harald Seidler, Ingenieurbüro Meinhart + Partner / Leopold Hauser
Construction period	2007–2008
Floor area	1.640 m^2
Gross area	2.047 m^2
Volume	7.691 m^3
Location	A-4880 St. Georgen, Attergau, Austria
Client	Stallinger Immobilien GmbH
Specialist design	merz kley partner GmbH, Meinhart Ingenieurbüro, Innotech GmbH & Co KG, Elplan Elmar Lingg, Erich Reiner Ingenieurbüro
Photographs	Werner Huthmacher

Building	Office and Residential Building Sportplatzweg
Architects / chief designers	Hermann Kaufmann, Christian Lenz
Assistants	Wolfgang Elmenreich, Peter Nußbaumer, Norbert Kaufmann, Elmar Gmeiner
Construction period	1998–1999
Floor area	1.390 m^2
Gross area	1.670 m^2
Location	Sportplatzweg 5, A-6858 Schwarzach, Vorarlberg, Austria
Client	Miterrichtergemeinschaft Kaufmann/Lenz/Gmeiner und Fa. Revital Bauträger GmbH
Specialist design	M+G Ingenieure, Statikbüro Galehr, Peter Naßwetter, Andreas Hecht, Lothar Künz ZT GmbH, Karl Brüstle, Barbara Bacher
Photographs	Ignacio Martinez

Building	Ludesch Community Centre
Architect / chief designer	Hermann Kaufmann
Assistants	Roland Wehinger, Martin Längle, Norbert Kaufmann
Construction period	2004–2005
Floor area	3.135 m^2
Volume	14.500 m^3
Location	Raiffeisenstraße 56, A-6713 Ludesch, Vorarlberg, Austria
Client	Gemeinde Ludesch, Immobilienverwaltungs GmbH & Co KEG
Specialist design	Mader & Flatz Ziviltechniker GmbH, merz kaufmann partner GmbH, Zementol VertriebsgesmbH, Synergy GmbH, Wilhelm Brugger, Bernhard Weithas, IBO / Karl Torghele
Photographs	Bruno Klomfar

Building	Sutterlüty Supermarket
Architect / chief designer	Hermann Kaufmann
Assistants	Stefan Hiebeler, Martin Rümmele, Norbert Kaufmann
Year of construction	2002
Floor area	1.314 m²
Gross area	1.412 m²
Volume	7.998 m³
Location	A-6833 Weiler, Vorarlberg, Austria
Client	Sutterlüty GesmbH & Co
Specialist design	Mader & Flatz Ziviltechniker GmbH, merz kaufmann partner GmnbH, Werner Dür GmbH, Hecht Andreas
Photographs	Bruno Klomfar

Building	Metzler Timber Warehouse and Offices and shed roof
Architect / chief designer	Hermann Kaufmann
Assistants	Jürgen Hagspiel, Wolfgang Elmenreich, Wolfgang Hammerer
Year of construction	1995
Floor area	1.800 m²
Gross area	1.900 m² / shed roof 3.000 m²
Volume	19.800 m³
Location	Wilbinger 566, A-6870 Bezau, Vorarlberg, Austria
Client	Metzler H. KG
Specialist design	Ingo Gehrer
Photographs	Bruno Klomfar, Ignacio Martinez (p. 86 top)

Building	Sohm Holzbau Office and Industrial Building, Extension
Architect / chief designer	Hermann Kaufmann
Assistants	Roland Wehinger, Johannes Grissmann, Christian Milz / Sohm Holzbautechnik GesmbH
Construction period	2008–2009
Floor area	612 m²
Gross area	warm 815 m² (1.300 m²)
Volume	warm 2.670 m³
Location	Bühel 818, A-6861 Alberschwende, Vorarlberg, Austria
Client	Sohm Holzbautechnik GesmbH
Specialist design	Sohm Holzbautechnik GesmbH
Photographs	Bruno Klomfar

Building   Wälderhaus Industrial Park
Architect / chief designer   Hermann Kaufmann
Assistants   Norbert Kaufmann, Simone Roos, Wolfgang Hammerer,
                                Norbert Kaufmann
Construction period   2001–2002
Floor area   5.464 m^2
Gross area   5.765 m^2
Volume   43.455 m^3
Location   Wilbinger 662, A-6870 Bezau, Vorarlberg, Austria
Client   Wälderhaus Immobilien GesmbH
Specialist design   Stefan Krauss, E-Plus, Willi Meusburger
Photographs   Ignacio Martinez

Building   Rheinhof Estate
Architect / chief designer   Hermann Kaufmann
Assistants   Landeshochbauamt, Martin Rümmele, Bmst.Gerold Hämmerle
Year of construction   2006
Floor area   1.462 m^2
Gross area   1.625m^2
Volume   9.830 m^3
Location   Rheinhof, A-6845 Hohenems, Vorarlberg, Austria
Client   Amt der Vorarlberger Landesregierung
Specialist design   merz kaufmann partner GmbH, Techn. Büro Ing. Stefan Amann,
                                Techn. Büro Manfred Seewald, Plankel, Pelzl & Partner GmbH
Photographs   Bruno Klomfar

Building   St. Gerold Riding Hall
Architect / chief designer   Hermann Kaufmann
Assistants   Wolfgang Elmenreich, Reinhard Muxel
Year of construction   1997
Floor area   800 m^2
Gross area   880 m^2
Volume   4.710 m^3
Location   Propstei St. Gerold, A-6721 St. Gerold, Vorarlberg, Austria
Client   Pater Nathanael Wirth, Propstei St. Gerold
Specialist design   merz kaufmann partner GmbH
Photographs   Ignacio Martinez

Building	Mehrerau Gymnasium, Conversion
Architect / chief designer	Hermann Kaufmann & Christian Lenz
Assistants	Rolf Ennulat, Nives Pavkovic
Construction period	1996–1997
Floor area	3.700 m^2
Gross area	4.500 m^2
Volume	20.100 m^3
Location	Mehrerauerstraße 68, A-6900 Bregenz, Vorarlberg, Austria
Client	Collegium Bernardi – Kloster Mehrerau
Specialist design	merz kaufmann partner GmbH, M+G Ingenieure, Josef Galehr, GMI Ingenieure, Hecht Elektroplanungsbüro, Lothar Künz ZT GmbH
Photographs	Bruno Klomfar

Building	Adler Inn, renovation
Architect / chief designer	Hermann Kaufmann
Assistants	Gerold Leuprecht
Year of construction	1991
Floor area	510 m^2
Gross area	610 m^2
Volume	1.400 m^3
Location	Hof 15, A-6867 Schwarzenberg, Vorarlberg, Austria
Client	Heidi and Engelbert Kaufmann
Specialist design	Ingo Gehrer, Hans Tschernig
Photographs	Adolf Bereuter

Building	Mesmer Stable, Conversion
Architect / chief designer	Hermann Kaufmann
Assistants	Norbert Kaufmann, Benjamin Baumgartl, Harald Seidler, Norbert Kaufmann
Year of construction	2004
Location	A-6861 Alberschwende, Vorarlberg, Austria
Client	Gemeinde Alberschwende
Photographs	Bruno Klomfar

COMPLETED PROJECTS

1989	Hittisau Community Center – Hittisau
1990	Dafins Solar-heated School – Dafins
1990	Kaufmann Michael Factory Hall – Reuthe
1991	Kaufmann Holz AG Warehouse – Reuthe
1993	Rieger Organ Factory – Schwarzach
1994	Glas Marte Factory Hall – Bregenz
1995	Linth Furniture Factory – Kaltbrunn, CH
1995	Murau Exhibition Hall – Murau
1997	Sonnenkopf Liftstation – Klösterle
1997	Raiffeisenbank – Bezau
1998	Greußinghof Stable and Single Family House– Lauterach
1998	Rheindeltahaus – Fußach
1998	Beck-Faigle Single Family House – Hard
1998	Kaufmann Anton Single Family House – Reuthe
1998	Klaus Community Center – Klaus
1999	Bizau Primary School – Bizau
2000	Kaufmann Holz AG Halle Au, Extension – Au
2000	Kopf Thomas Single Family House – Au
2000	Impuls Center – Egg
2001	Dobler Carpentry and Office – Röthis
2001	Fuchs Reinhard Single Family House – Langen / Bregenz
2001	Die Drei Office – Dornbirn
2002	Schnepfau Town Center – Schnepfau
2002	Moosmann Petra Single Family House – Lauterach

2002	Dorner Electronic – Egg
2003	Schwarz Gerhard Double Family House – Schwarzenberg
2004	Housing Estate Hofsteigstraße – Wolfurt
2004	Sutterlüty Supermarket Rohrbach – Dornbirn
2005	Mathis Aiga and Reinhard Single Family House – Dafins
2005	Pfadfinderheim – Wolfurt
2005	Kessler Sieglinde and Klaus Single Family House – Hirschegg
2006	Village Center – Schwarzach
2006	Mohren Pavilion – Dornbirn
2007	Sutterlüty City Park Supermarket and Housing Estate – Dornbirn
2007	Strolz Hubert Stable – Warth
2007	Housing Estate Allmeinteilweg
2007	Rinner Edith and Reinhold Single Family House Renovation – Egg
2008	Chesa Valisa - Hotel Renovation and Extension - Hirschegg
2008	Rheinhof – Single Family Housing, Hohenems
2009	Schwanen Bizau Hotel Renovation – Bizau
2010	Kindergarten – Garching (D)
2010	Raiffeisenbank – Egg
2010	Chanteloup Hostel and Convention House - Chanteloup les Vignes, Paris (F)

PROJECT TEXT TRANSLATIONS

House Zerlauth, Olperer Hut, Elma Alp Vacation Home, Mühlweg Housing Estate, MM Immobilien St. Georgen GmbH Offices, Ludesch Community Centre, Sutterlüty Supermarket, Wälderhaus Industrial Park, Rheinhof Estate, Mesmers Stable, conversion: *Hermann Kaufmann Wood Works*, Springer Verlag, Wien 2009 / Andrea Lyman, Mark Gilbert (German–English); Outi Leinonen (English–Finnish)

Ölzbündt Housing Estate, St. Gerold Riding Hall, Mehrerau Gymnasium, conversion: *Hermann Kaufmann, Christian Lenz Architectur und Structur,* Springer Verlag, Wien–New York 2002 / Pedro M. López (German-English); Outi Leinonen (English–Finnish

Bicycle Bridge, Office and Residential Building Sportplatzweg, Metzler Timber Warehouse and Offices, Adler Inn, renovation: Josbel Oy (German–Finnish), Gekko / Gareth Griffiths, Kristina Kölhi (Finnish–English)